Indian
BIBLE

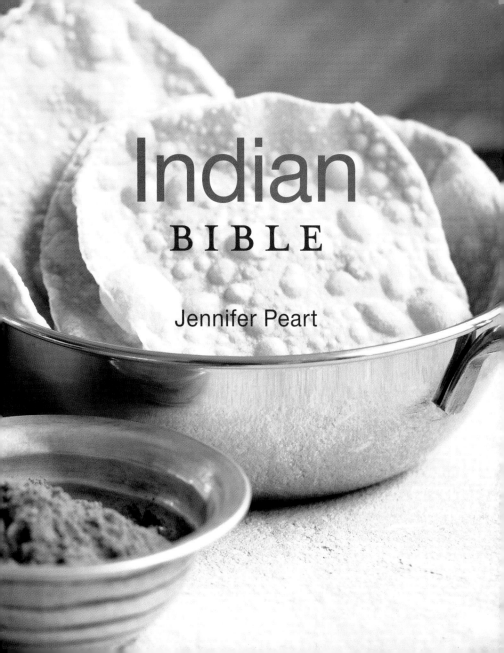

Indian

BIBLE

Jennifer Peart

Contents

Introduction

Indian food is as complex and diverse as the country itself, with dishes heavily influenced by regional factors. In the arid north, pulses and breads feature prominently, while in the south, fresh seafood, rice and coconut are the main players.

The unique flavours of Indian cuisine come from the blending of aromatic spices and herbs, such as cinnamon, saffron, cloves and coriander. Chilli is a ubiquitous ingredient – but that doesn't mean every dish is hot. There are dishes to suit every palate, from mild, creamy kormas to eye-wateringly fiery vindaloos.

Meals are often quick and easy to prepare, and immensely satisfying. The country also boasts arguably the world's greatest array of vegetarian dishes, often based around legumes such as lentils, chickpeas and red kidney beans.

Indian Basics

Many people associate Indian food with hot curries, but it is in fact an amazingly varied cuisine, as might be expected of such a vast and ethnically diverse continent. Religious beliefs and practices also have a profound influence on the Indian diet and kitchen: as the cow is sacred to Hindus, eating beef is prohibited; for Muslims, pork is forbidden; and most branches of Buddhism advocate vegetarianism (although meat-eating is not specifically forbidden in its scriptures).

Indian dishes range from mildly spiced to fiery, from creamy to dry-fried or grilled, from sour to sweet, but they all have one common characteristic: a carefully selected blend of spices that may be unique to particular households, districts or regions. While the list of ingredients for some dishes may seem long, pantry basics such as garlic, onion, chillies and ginger, and just a few key spices, are enough to get you started.

The people of India are careful to balance heating and cooling foods in their diet: yoghurt, rice and ghee are considered cooling and are therefore consumed mostly in warmer months; meat, nuts and mangoes are considered heat-inducing.

The Indian Table

Indian meals are traditionally laid out buffet-style, with a range of dishes from which diners serve themselves. You can, of course, offer successive courses, western-style, if you prefer.

A typical Indian meal is likely to consist of at least two main dishes (typically one 'wet' curry and one 'dry' curry, and one or more vegetable dishes), light foods such as pakoras, rice and/or breads, salads or yoghurt dishes, and chutneys and pickles. For a simple home meal there will be only a few different dishes offered; while for elaborate parties or festivals there will be more variety, and expensive ingredients such as saffron, nuts and dried fruits will be featured.

With an estimated 30–40 per cent of the population being vegetarian, there are countless delicious dishes based on legumes and seasonal vegetables. Dairy products and eggs are eaten by many vegetarians in India, with yoghurt and paneer (a simple curd-style cheese) providing an important source of protein.

A TYPICAL MENU

A characteristic North Indian 'banquet' menu:

- Spicy Potato Bread (Aloo Paratha) (page 60)
- Yellow & White Rice (page 52)
- Fried Potato Patties (Aloo Tikki) (page 100)
- Creamy Black Lentils (Dal Makhani) (page 104)
- Chickpea Dish from North India (Chana Kadai) (page 113)
- Spicy Goat Curry (Raarha Ghosht) (page 190)
- Fish Curry from Hyderabad (page 118)
- Pumpkin Curry (page 79)
- Spicy Okra (page 92)
- Kidney-bean Curry (page 110)
- Kashmiri Chicken (page 142)
- Mango Chutney (page 233)

- Paneer with Peas & Spices (Mattar Paneer) (page 94)
- Pistachio Lassi (page 223)
- Besan Burfi (page 218)
- Carrot Halwa (page 210)

Regional Ingredients & Flavours

Each region of the vast Asian 'subcontinent' of India is distinctive geographically, historically and culturally. The landscape includes the world's highest mountains, as well as lowland floodplains, desert, wetlands and coasts. The nation has been governed by many different groups, including the ancient Persians and Greeks, the French, the Portuguese and several Muslim empires as well as the British. So it is not surprising that the food varies greatly from north to south, east to west, state to state, village to village, household to household. Dal dishes are a good example of this: a South Indian dal is likely to be flavoured with fenugreek, curry leaves and tamarind; while in Mumbai it will include tomatoes and fresh coriander.

South Indian cuisine is famous for its rice, vegetables and seafood. Fresh coconuts are plentiful, so coconut milk is used in many dishes. Bengal is noted for its fiery seafood dishes and tooth-achingly sweet desserts. The Portuguese retained the southern port of Goa for three centuries, until 1965, so their influence on the cooking of that region is strong – particularly in the use of vinegar.

North Indian cuisine is much influenced by Persian and Turkish flavours and cooking techniques, such as cooking with yoghurt and adding dried fruit and nuts to meat dishes. The elaborate biryani originated among Muslims here. Also in the north is the state of Uttar Pradesh, which is predominantly Hindu. Its food is simple, lightly spiced and vegetarian. Kashmir is known for its rich meat dishes, particularly lamb.

SPICES & SPICE MIXES

Spices are the heart and soul of Indian cooking and knowing how to use them is the key to producing delicious Indian meals.

For maximum freshness, buy whole spices (such as cumin and coriander seeds) whenever possible. Most recipes require you to toast the spices before use, to release their flavours and eliminate any raw taste: toast them in a dry frying pan, allow to cool, then crush in a mortar and pestle or a spice grinder. Be careful not to cook them for too long, as they can burn or become bitter.

There are several key spices that are common to many Indian dishes, such as chilli, coriander, cumin and turmeric. Onions, ginger and garlic also used very widely. While spicy, Indian food is not necessarily hot; generally curries that feature yoghurt or coconut milk are

Prepared spice mixes and pastes, such as tandoori, are now readily available in supermarkets and Indian grocery stores. However, it is not difficult or time-consuming to make your own (you'll find recipes for chana masala spice mix and several curry pastes in the Extras section).

Equipment & Techniques

You don't need any special equipment to cook Indian food, although a spice/coffee grinder or mortar and pestle are invaluable for crushing spices. A food processor with a small bowl comes in very handy for grinding 'wet' pastes such as onion, ginger and garlic.

One or two frying pans or woks are also essential: a small one for frying spices; a larger, preferably heavy-based, one for cooking whole dishes. The traditional Indian version, called a kadai, is a two-handled wok-like pan. A flat griddle pan (in India called a tava) is perfect for cooking Indian breads. An electric rice cooker is also a good investment if you cook Indian food often.

When you're cooking kebabs or other skewered dishes, you can use metal or bamboo skewers. If using metal skewers, choose the square-edged type, as they hold the ingredients (especially meat) more successfully and will not roll around on the grill. Bamboo skewers should be soaked in water for at least 20 minutes before threading, to prevent them burning.

Some Indian Staples

CHILLIES

There are hundreds of varieties of chillies and colour is no guide to their heat factor.

Generally, green chillies in India have a hot fresh taste while red ones have a sweeter, more robust flavour. (Note that green chillies bought in Australia are often mild.) Small red chillies are much hotter than large ones. Dried chillies tend to have a more intense flavour than fresh ones but are not necessarily hotter. Try to find red or green Indian chillies (sometimes called finger chillies) or Thai chillies for Indian dishes. Mexican chillies have a different flavour and are not recommended.

For a milder dish, add chillies whole and remove them before the end of the cooking time; the longer a chilli stays in a dish, the hotter it will be. Deseeding chillies before using them is another way to reduce their heat.

Always wash your hands well with soap and water, or rub a little cooking oil into your hands, after handling chillies. Or wear rubber gloves to prepare them.

COCONUT

The firm flesh of a fresh coconut is used in some recipes: to extract it, simply crack open the coconut and cut out the white flesh.

Canned coconut milk and cream are widely available, and are easy and convenient to use. Made fresh, though, these ingredients add an amazing taste to dishes, particularly seafood.

To use fresh coconut **to make coconut milk or cream**, blend the flesh in a food processor with a little water (this gives you coconut cream, which should be added late in the cooking process); or thin it further with more water and process again, to achieve the thinner coconut milk that can withstand longer cooking times.

You can also use desiccated coconut to make coconut milk: for 2 cups (500 ml/17 fl oz) coconut milk, blend 1½ cups desiccated coconut with 3 cups (750 ml/25 fl oz) hot water (use 2 cups hot water and 1 cup milk for a creamier consistency).

GHEE AND OIL

Ghee is a golden, nutty-flavoured form of clarified butter, which keeps well and won't burn at high temperatures. Ghee is easy to find in supermarkets, but it's not too hard to make your own. **To make ghee**, melt 250 g (9 oz) unsalted butter in a heavy-based saucepan over low–medium heat until all the water has

evaporated and the solids have settled to the bottom (about 30 minutes). Carefully pour the liquid top layer into a container, leaving the solids behind.

Vegetable, sunflower and corn oil can be substituted for ghee in most Indian recipes, except desserts. Olive oil generally isn't used in Indian cooking. Mustard oil is used to make pickles and chutneys – it is preheated almost to the point of smoking before use, to get rid of the pungent taste and smell.

PANEER
You can buy this cottage-style cheese at Indian food stores and many supermarkets.

To make your own paneer, bring 1 litre (34 fl oz) full-cream milk to the boil, then remove from the heat. Stir in 1 tablespoon (20 ml/¾ fl oz) freshly squeezed lemon juice (or use vinegar) until the milk separates into solids (the cheese) and liquid (whey). Leave to stand for a few minutes, then strain very carefully through a piece of muslin or a very fine sieve. Place resulting cheese on a plate and weight it with a heavy object for a few hours, until all the liquid has drained away. Refrigerate, and use within 3–4 days.

RICE

The most popular rice in India is basmati, which has long, slim grains that are fluffy and separate when cooked. It is generally recommended that basmati rice be rinsed before cooking, to remove excess starch.

To make plain boiled rice, wash 1 cup rice, add 2 cups (500 ml/17 fl oz) water and bring to the boil over high heat. As soon as it starts to boil, lower heat, half cover the pan and simmer for 10 minutes. Stir lightly with a fork to separate the grains, then put lid on and cook over low heat for another 2–3 minutes. Remove from heat and set aside, still covered, for 10 minutes.

YOGHURT

Natural (plain) yoghurt is best for Indian cooking. It is added to curries and sauces to give a creamy texture, and is also used as a souring agent. Yoghurt should be lightly whisked with a fork to a smooth consistency before use. Yoghurt will curdle quickly when heated and needs to be stirred in well when added to a dish.

Thickening yoghurt by draining away the liquid (whey) gives it a creamier texture. **To drain yoghurt**, place a coffee-filter paper, or a piece of muslin or cheesecloth, in a fine sieve, add the yoghurt and set over a bowl. Place in the fridge to drain overnight.

Snacks & Light Dishes

Generally in India there is no concept of starters or entrées at the beginning of a meal, as all dishes are usually laid out at once. Soups are uncommon and are most likely to be served as one of the 'wet' dishes in a meal, or perhaps as a complete meal (particularly breakfast), rather than as a first course in the western tradition.

The small foods in this section, such as samosas and bhajis, might be passed around with drinks before a meal, served as part of a light meal, or enjoyed as a snack at just about any time of day. Many of the dishes here, like the Amritsar fish and the chicken tikkas, are popular street foods.

‹ Vegetable Pakoras (page 20)

Vegetable Pakoras

Serves 4–6

vegetable oil for deep-frying

2 large potatoes, peeled and cut into 5-mm slices

½ small cauliflower, separated into florets

2 cups (300 g/10½ oz) besan (chickpea flour)

½ teaspoon baking powder

½ teaspoon salt

1 eggplant, cut into 5-mm slices

tomato chutney (page 234), to serve

Preheat the vegetable oil in a deep frying pan or wok. Blanch the potatoes and cauliflower in boiling water until not quite tender.

Mix the flour, baking powder and salt in a bowl, and gradually add about 1 cup (250 ml/8½ fl oz) water, to make a thick batter.

Dip prepared vegetables into the batter, one piece at a time, then deep-fry in batches for 1–2 minutes until golden-brown.

Drain on paper towels and serve hot with tomato chutney.

Other vegetables that could be used to make pakoras include zucchini, carrots, mushrooms and beans.

Spicy Potatoes

Serves 4

⅓ cup (80 ml/3 fl oz)
   vegetable oil

4 cloves garlic, crushed

1 teaspoon cumin seeds

6 large potatoes, peeled
   and cut into thin chips
   (French fries)

salt and freshly ground
   black pepper

1 teaspoon ground chilli

Heat the oil in a large frying pan, add the garlic and cumin seeds, and fry for 30 seconds. Add the potatoes and stir-fry until translucent, then add the salt, pepper and chilli, and mix well. Cook over a low heat, stirring frequently, until the potatoes are tender (about 10 minutes).

Drain on paper towels and serve hot.

Chicken Tikka

Serves 6–8

2.5-cm (1-in) piece fresh ginger, grated

3 cloves garlic, crushed

1 small fresh hot green chilli, chopped

½ cup chopped fresh coriander leaves, plus extra leaves for garnish

2 tablespoons (40 ml/1½ fl oz) vegetable oil

¼ cup (60 ml/2 fl oz) plain yoghurt

½ teaspoon salt

1 tablespoon (20 ml/¾ fl oz) freshly squeezed lemon juice

2 teaspoons tandoori masala (page 239)

1 teaspoon garam masala

4 skinless chicken breast fillets, cut into 5-cm (2-in) pieces

lemon wedges, to serve

If using bamboo skewers, soak them in water for at least 20 minutes before threading, to prevent them burning.

Put the ginger, garlic, chilli and chopped coriander in a food processor and blend to a paste (or use a mortar and pestle). Transfer to a large bowl and add the oil, yoghurt, salt, lemon juice, tandoori and garam masalas, and mix well. Add the chicken pieces to the bowl and spoon the marinade over. Cover, and chill for at least 1 hour, turning occasionally.

Preheat grill or barbecue to medium–hot.

Drain the chicken pieces (reserve the marinade) and thread onto skewers. Grill for 10–12 minutes, basting with the marinade and turning skewers frequently to ensure the chicken is cooked through.

Remove the cooked chicken from the skewers and place on a serving plate. Garnish with lemon wedges and fresh coriander, and serve immediately.

For variety, capsicum, mushroom and onion slices can be added to the skewers.

Sambar-style Spicy Soup

Serves 4

2 tablespoons (40 ml/1½ fl oz)
  vegetable oil

3 cloves garlic, crushed

½ teaspoon freshly ground
  black pepper

½ teaspoon black
  mustard seeds

1 teaspoon cumin seeds

2 dried red chillies

½ teaspoon ground turmeric

½ teaspoon asafoetida

4 curry leaves

1 cup (250 ml/8½ fl oz)
  tomato juice

juice of 2 lemons

1 teaspoon salt

chopped fresh coriander,
  for garnish

Heat the oil in a large saucepan and fry the garlic, pepper, mustard seeds, cumin seeds and whole red chillies. Add the turmeric, asafoetida and curry leaves, and cook over medium heat for 5 minutes until the garlic is golden-brown.

Lower the heat and add the tomato juice, lemon juice and ½ cup (125 ml/ 4 fl oz) water. Bring to the boil then simmer for 10 minutes. Add the salt, remove the whole red chillies and garnish with the chopped coriander.

Chilli Pakoras

Serves 8

20 long fresh mild green
  chillies
1½ cups unsalted peanuts
1 teaspoon tamarind paste
½ teaspoon salt
oil for deep-frying

SPICY BATTER
1½ cups (225 g/8 oz) besan
  (chickpea flour)
pinch of bicarbonate of soda
1 teaspoon grated fresh ginger
1 teaspoon crushed garlic
½ teaspoon salt
½ teaspoon ground chilli

Cut the tip off each chilli, then slit lengthways down the middle, without splitting the chilli open (leave the stalk-end intact). Remove the seeds with a small knife.

Toast the peanuts for a few minutes in a dry frying pan. Place in a blender with the tamarind paste, salt and 2 tablespoons (40 ml/1½ fl oz) water, and grind to a thick paste. Fill each chilli with about 1 teaspoon of the peanut mixture, making sure the chilli stays in one piece.

To make the batter, simply place all the ingredients in a large bowl and mix together. Gradually add 1 cup (250 ml/8½ fl oz) cold water and stir until smooth and thick. Carefully dip each filled chilli into the batter and turn to coat well.

Heat the oil over medium heat in a pan suitable for deep-frying. Cook pakoras until nicely browned (approximately 5 minutes). Drain on paper towels, then serve immediately.

ॐ Make sure to choose mild chillies for this dish, or the chilli heat will be overwhelming.

Indian Spicy Omelette

Poro

Serves 2–3

1 small potato

3 eggs

salt and freshly ground
  black pepper

½ teaspoon ground chilli

2 tablespoons (40 ml/1½ fl oz)
  melted ghee

1 small onion, finely chopped

1 small fresh hot green chilli,
  deseeded and finely chopped

¼ cup cooked peas

¼ cup grated cheddar cheese

fresh coriander leaves,
  for garnish

Boil the potato until tender, then peel and dice finely.

Preheat grill to hot.

Beat the eggs until frothy, then mix in the salt, pepper and ground chilli.

Heat the ghee in a large frying pan over medium heat. Pour in the egg mixture, reduce heat and sprinkle in the onion, fresh chilli, potato cubes and peas. When surface is set, gently turn omelette over and sprinkle with the cheese.

Place pan under preheated grill and cook until cheese has melted. Cut into slices and serve immediately, garnished with coriander leaves.

❧ You will need a pan about 15 cm (6 in) in diameter for this omelette.

Amritsar Fish

Serves 4

2 cloves garlic, crushed

1 teaspoon ground turmeric

1 teaspoon ground coriander

1 teaspoon cumin seeds

1 teaspoon ground chilli

⅓ cup (80 ml/3 fl oz) freshly squeezed lemon juice, plus extra to serve

600 g (1 lb 5 oz) firm white fish, cut into 2.5-cm (1-in) chunks

⅓ cup (50 g/1¾ oz) rice flour

¾ cup (180 ml/6 fl oz) vegetable oil, for deep-frying

salt

Mix the garlic and spices with the lemon juice in a small bowl. Place fish pieces in a large shallow dish, pour the lemon–spice mixture over and stir. Marinate for at least 1 hour in the refrigerator.

When ready to cook, remove fish from the marinade and pat dry with paper towels. Coat fish with the rice flour.

Heat vegetable oil in a pan suitable for deep-frying and fry the fish in batches for about 5 minutes, until golden-brown and cooked through. Drain on paper towels, sprinkle with salt and extra lemon juice, and serve hot.

Eggplant Dip

Baigan bharta

Serves 4

1 large eggplant

about 2½ tablespoons (50 ml/ 1¾ fl oz) vegetable oil

1 teaspoon cumin seeds

1 medium-sized onion, chopped

4 cloves garlic, crushed

¼ teaspoon ground turmeric

1 teaspoon ground chilli

1 teaspoon garam masala

1 teaspoon salt

½ cup cooked peas

1 tomato, finely chopped

naan (page 53), to serve

Preheat oven to 180°C (360°F), or barbecue or grill to hot.

Rub the eggplant all over with a little of the vegetable oil. Roast, barbecue or grill the eggplant for 45 minutes or until flesh is soft. Leave to cool, then peel and chop flesh roughly. Mash and set aside.

Heat remaining oil in a pan and fry the cumin seeds over medium heat for a few seconds. Add onion and garlic, and stir until soft and golden.

Mix the turmeric, chilli, garam masala and salt into the onion mixture. Add the peas and tomato, cover the pan and cook for 5 minutes until the tomato has softened. Add mashed eggplant to the pan and mix thoroughly. Cook for 5 minutes over medium heat, until mixture reduces and thickens.

Serve the dip warm, with toasted naan bread.

Onion Bhajis

Serves 6

1 egg

1 tablespoon (20 ml/¾ fl oz)
freshly squeezed lemon juice

1¼ cups (175 g/6½ oz)
plain flour

1 teaspoon salt

1 teaspoon ground cumin

1 teaspoon ground turmeric

1 teaspoon ground chilli

¼ teaspoon asafoetida

1 teaspoon garam masala

¾ cup (180 ml/6 fl oz)
vegetable oil

2 onions, thinly sliced

1 cup chopped fresh
coriander leaves

1 small fresh hot green chilli,
deseeded and finely chopped

lemon wedges, to serve

Whisk the egg, lemon juice and ⅔ cup (160 ml/5 fl oz) cold water in a bowl.

Sift the flour, salt and spices into a separate bowl. Make a well in the centre, pour in the egg mixture and mix it gradually into the flour, using a fork, until you have a thick batter.

Heat the oil to hot in a large frying pan.

Meanwhile, stir the onions, coriander and chopped chilli into the batter. Carefully slide spoonfuls of the mixture into the hot oil, a few at a time, and cook for 4 minutes, turning frequently, until brown on all sides.

Drain bhajis on paper towels and serve immediately, with lemon wedges.

Samosas

Makes 8–10

oil for deep-frying

fresh coriander relish
(page 226), to serve

DOUGH

2 cups (300 g/10½ oz)
plain flour

pinch of salt

3 tablespoons (60 ml/2 fl oz)
chilled vegetable oil

FILLING

6 potatoes

2 tablespoons (40 ml/1½ fl oz)
melted ghee

1 teaspoon cumin seeds

1 cup fresh or frozen peas

1 teaspoon salt

½ teaspoon ground turmeric

1 tablespoon grated
fresh ginger

½ teaspoon ground chilli

To prepare the dough, mix together the sifted flour, salt and oil. Gradually
add ½ cup (125 ml/4 fl oz) water and knead into quite a firm dough (add
a little more flour if necessary), then set aside while you prepare the filling.

For the filling, boil the potatoes until tender, then drain and cut into very
small cubes. Melt the ghee in a large frying pan over medium heat, then
sauté the cumin seeds for 1 minute. Add the potatoes and peas, give everything a good stir, add the salt and spices, and cook for a few minutes. Set
aside to cool. >

Divide the dough into 8–10 balls of equal size. Roll each out to a round about 20 cm (8 in) in diameter. Cut each circle in half, brush the straight edge with water and form dough into a cone. Place a tablespoonful of the filling in each cone, draw down the top flap and seal the edges, pressing tightly.

Heat the oil over medium heat in a wok or other pan suitable for deep-frying, and deep-fry the samosas in batches of three or four until golden (around 5 minutes).

Drain on paper towels and serve hot with fresh coriander relish.

Seekh Kebabs

Serves 6–8

1 tablespoon (20 ml/¾ fl oz) vegetable oil

1 onion, finely chopped

750 g (1 lb 10 oz) lamb mince

5-cm (2-in) piece fresh ginger

3 cloves garlic, crushed

1 small fresh hot green chilli, finely chopped

2 tablespoons chopped fresh coriander

1 teaspoon ground chilli

1 teaspoon garam masala

2 teaspoons ground coriander

1 teaspoon ground cumin

1 teaspoon salt

1 egg, beaten

cucumber raita (page 227), to serve

Heat oil in a small pan, fry the onion until softened, then set aside to cool.

In a food processor, blend the cooked onion with the lamb, ginger, garlic, fresh chilli and coriander, spices and salt. Gradually add the egg. Refrigerate mixture for at least 1 hour.

Preheat grill to hot.

With wet hands, form the lamb mixture into golfball-sized balls. Thread three or four at a time onto metal skewers. Grill the kebabs for 10 minutes, turning occasionally, until they are browned on all sides.

Serve with cucumber raita.

Bengali Masala Prawns

Serves 4–6

20–24 raw (green) tiger prawns, shelled but head and tail left on

1 teaspoon garam masala

juice of ½ lemon

½ teaspoon salt

2½ tablespoons (50 ml/1¾ fl oz) vegetable oil

1 large onion, thinly sliced

8 cloves garlic, crushed

2.5-cm (1-in) piece fresh ginger, grated

1 small fresh hot green chilli, slit open

2 tomatoes, chopped

1 tablespoon fresh coriander leaves, plus extra for garnish

1 teaspoon crushed coriander seeds

½ teaspoon dried red chilli flakes

lemon wedges, for garnish

Place the prawns in a bowl with the garam masala, lemon juice and salt, and marinate for 1 hour.

Heat oil in a frying pan and fry the onion, garlic, ginger and fresh chilli until onion is golden-brown. Add tomatoes and fresh coriander, and cook for 2 minutes, then add coriander seeds and chilli flakes, and cook for another minute. Add prawns to the pan with their marinade, mix well and cover. Lower the heat and simmer for 4–5 minutes, until prawns are cooked.

Serve hot, garnished with extra coriander and lemon wedges.

Rice & Bread

Rice or bread (sometimes both) is served with pretty well every Indian meal. Wheat is grown in the north, so bread tends to be the daily staple there; while the major rice-growing provinces are in South India.

Plain basmati rice is a perfect accompaniment for most curries. It is also delicious when made into a pulao (called pilaf or pilav in Europe and the Middle East), for which the rice is lightly fried and then cooked with vegetables, herbs and spices. A more festive version is the biryani, where rice is layered with meat and/or vegetables, and garnished with nuts and dried fruits.

In Indian homes, bread is usually made fresh for each meal. Most Indian breads are unleavened, and quick and easy to make. They are typically matched carefully with the main dish: a rich North Indian meat dish might be served with plain grilled chapatis, while a simple potato dish might be embellished with deep-fried pooris.

< Kitcheree (page 42)

Kitcheree

Serves 4

1 cup basmati rice

2 tablespoons (40 ml/1½ fl oz) melted ghee

1 onion, finely chopped

1 small fresh hot green chilli, chopped

1 cup split red lentils (masoor dal), rinsed

¼ teaspoon asafoetida

1 teaspoon salt

½ teaspoon garam masala

2 tablespoons chopped fresh coriander

Rinse the rice, then soak for 30 minutes in about 1 cup cold water. Drain and set aside.

Heat the ghee in a heavy-based pan and fry the onion and green chilli for 5 minutes, until onion is golden. Add the rice, lentils, asafoetida, salt and garam masala, and stir for 2 minutes.

Add 3 cups (750 ml/1½ pt) water to the pan and bring to the boil, stirring. Reduce the heat, cover pan and simmer for 20 minutes (without lifting the lid), until the grains are tender and the liquid absorbed. Remove from the heat and leave to stand for 5 minutes.

Stir in the fresh coriander and serve warm.

Coconut Rice

Serves 6

1¾ cups basmati rice
400 ml (13 fl oz) coconut milk
½ teaspoon salt
1 teaspoon sugar
½ teaspoon ground turmeric
pinch of saffron threads

Place rice in a bowl, cover with cold water and soak for 30 minutes. Rinse and drain.

Place rice in a heavy-based saucepan with 1¼ cups (310 ml/10½ fl oz) water, the coconut milk and remaining ingredients. Bring to the boil, stirring occasionally, then reduce heat and simmer, covered, for 15 minutes or until rice is tender.

Remove from heat and stand for 10 minutes with the lid on. Serve warm.

Indian-style Fried Rice

Serves 4

3 tablespoons (60 ml/2 fl oz)
  vegetable oil

10 curry leaves

1 onion, sliced

3 green cardamom
  pods, bruised

2 small fresh hot green
  chillies, sliced

5 cloves garlic, crushed

200 g (7 oz) raw (green)
  prawns, shelled

1 cup shredded cabbage

1½ cups grated carrot

1 tablespoon crushed chilli

salt and freshly ground
  black pepper

2 tablespoons (40 ml/1½ fl oz)
  dark soy sauce

2 tablespoons (40 ml/1½ fl oz)
  light soy sauce

2 cups cooked basmati rice

1 cup cooked peas

1 cup chopped fresh
  coriander leaves,
  plus extra for garnish

1 egg, fried and cut into strips

Heat oil in a wok and add the curry leaves, onion, cardamom, fresh chillies and garlic. Sauté for a few minutes until the onion has softened. Add the prawns, cabbage and carrot to the wok, stir well and then add the chilli paste, salt and pepper, and the soy sauces.

Add cooked rice to wok, turn up the heat and quickly toss the ingredients to mix. Sprinkle in the peas and heat through. Remove cardamom pods and serve the rice hot, garnished with the egg strips and some extra coriander.

Basmati Rice with Peas

Matar pulao

Serves 4

1 cup basmati rice

2 tablespoons (40 ml/1½ fl oz) vegetable oil

½ teaspoon cumin seeds

1 small onion, sliced

2 cloves

1 cinnamon stick

2 cups fresh or frozen (defrosted) peas

1 teaspoon salt

½ cup chopped toasted cashews

Place rice in a bowl, cover generously with cold water and soak for about 30 minutes. Rinse and drain.

In a heavy-based saucepan, heat the oil and fry the cumin seeds until they start to pop. Add onion and fry until golden, then add the cloves, cinnamon, peas and drained rice, and stir well. Add salt and 2 cups (500 ml/17 fl oz) water, cover and cook over low heat for 20 minutes or until rice is tender.

Garnish with chopped cashews.

Saffron Rice

Serves 4

1⅓ cups basmati rice

2½ cups (625 ml/18 fl oz) chicken or vegetable stock

pinch of saffron threads

2 tablespoons (40 ml/1½ fl oz) melted ghee

1 teaspoon cumin seeds

1 onion, finely chopped

2 cloves garlic, crushed

1 cinnamon stick

½ teaspoon ground turmeric

6 green cardamom pods, bruised

1 Indian bay leaf

½ cup sultanas

½ cup toasted unsalted cashews

CRISP-FRIED SHALLOTS

3 tablespoons (60 ml/2 fl oz) vegetable oil

5 shallots, sliced

To make the crisp-fried shallots, heat the vegetable oil in a frying pan over medium heat and fry the shallots until they are a deep golden-brown colour (5–6 minutes), making sure they don't burn. Drain on paper towels.

Place the rice in a bowl, cover generously with cold water and soak for about 30 minutes. Rinse and drain. >

In a saucepan, heat the stock with the saffron over medium heat.

Meanwhile, heat ghee in a large saucepan, add the cumin seeds and cook for a few minutes, until they start to pop. Add the onion and garlic, stirring until the onion softens, then add the cinnamon, turmeric, cardamom and bay leaf, and cook for a further 2 minutes. Add drained rice to the pan and stir for 2 minutes over low heat. Pour in the stock and the sultanas, and simmer, covered, for 10 minutes or until rice is tender and the liquid absorbed.

Fluff up the rice with a fork and remove the bay leaf and cinnamon stick before serving. Garnish with the cashews and crisp-fried shallots.

Spiced Basmati Rice

Serves 4

1 cup basmati rice

2 tablespoons (40 ml/1½ fl oz) melted ghee

5 green cardamom pods, bruised

5 cloves

1 cinnamon stick

1 teaspoon fennel seeds

½ teaspoon black mustard seeds

2 Indian bay leaves

1 teaspoon salt

2 cups (500 ml/17 fl oz) hot water

freshly ground black pepper

Place the rice in a bowl, cover generously with cold water and soak for 30 minutes. Rinse and drain.

Heat the ghee in a large saucepan over medium heat, add the cardamom, cloves, cinnamon, fennel and mustard seeds, and bay leaves, and stir-fry for 30 seconds. Add the drained rice to the pan and stir well until the rice is coated with the ghee. Stir in salt and water and bring to the boil.

Reduce heat, cover pan and simmer for 8–10 minutes until rice is tender and all the liquid absorbed. Turn off the heat and fluff up the rice with a fork, removing the cinnamon stick and bay leaves. Season with pepper, and more salt if needed.

Basmati Rice with Tomatoes

Tamatar pulao

Serves 4

1 cup basmati rice

2 tablespoons (40 ml/1½ fl oz) sunflower oil

1 teaspoon caraway seeds

1 teaspoon black peppercorns

10 curry leaves

2 tomatoes, chopped

⅓ cup (80 ml/3 fl oz) tomato purée

½ teaspoon salt

2 cups (500 ml/17 fl oz) hot water

½ cup chopped fresh coriander leaves

Place rice in a bowl, cover generously with cold water and soak for about 30 minutes. Rinse and drain.

Heat the oil in a heavy-based pan and stir-fry the caraway seeds and peppercorns until fragrant. Add the curry leaves and drained rice, reduce heat and fry for 5 minutes, stirring, until the rice grains are coated with oil. Add the tomatoes, tomato purée and salt, and mix well.

Increase the heat, pour hot water into the pan and stir well. Cover and cook over a low heat until rice is cooked and all the liquid absorbed (about 20 minutes). Serve garnished with coriander leaves.

Yellow & White Rice

Serves 4–6

2 cups basmati rice

pinch of saffron threads (or ½ teaspoon ground turmeric)

pinch of salt

Place rice in a bowl, cover generously with cold water and soak for about 30 minutes. Rinse and drain.

Place the saffron or turmeric in about 1 tablespoon hot water and leave to infuse while you prepare the rice.

Place rinsed rice in a heavy-based pan and add enough cold water to come 2 cm (¾ in) above the rice. Add salt, stir once, and bring to the boil. Reduce the heat, cover, and cook for 12–15 minutes without lifting the lid.

Remove rice from heat and leave to stand for 10 minutes, then fluff up with a fork. Divide cooked rice into two portions. Stir the saffron or turmeric water into one portion until uniformly yellow and set aside for a few minutes.

Mix the yellow rice through the uncoloured rice and serve on a flat dish.

Naan

Makes 12

500 g (1 lb 2 oz)
  self-raising flour

½ teaspoon salt

2 tablespoons (40 ml/1½ fl oz)
  vegetable oil, plus extra for
  rolling

2 cups (500 ml/17 fl oz)
  plain yoghurt

3 tablespoons milk
  (60 ml/2 fl oz)

2 tablespoons (40 ml/1½ fl oz)
  melted butter or ghee

Sift the flour and salt into a bowl. Mix in the oil, then add the yoghurt gradually and mix with your hands to make a soft dough. With oiled hands, form the dough into a large ball, return it to the bowl, cover with a damp tea towel and set aside in a warm place for 5–6 hours.

With oiled hands, divide dough into 12 balls. On a greased surface, roll out each ball to an oblong about 12 cm (5 in) long and 5 cm (2 in) wide.

Preheat grill to high. Heat a large, ungreased frying pan over medium heat. Cook naan, one at a time, for about a minute. Once the underside is browned, slide naan onto a tray with uncooked side facing up and place under the grill for 1–2 minutes until browned. Brush each naan with melted butter or ghee and keep warm in a tea towel until ready to serve.

⌁ Sesame seeds, chilli flakes, onion seeds or fresh coriander can be sprinkled on top of the naan before grilling.

Chapatis

Makes 16

400 g (14 oz) chapati flour (atta), plus extra for dusting

1 teaspoon salt

½ teaspoon sugar

2 tablespoons (40 ml/1½ fl oz) vegetable oil

2 tablespoons (40 ml/1½ fl oz) melted ghee or butter, to serve (optional)

Mix the sifted flour, salt and sugar together in a large bowl. Add the oil and use your fingers to mix it into the flour. Gradually add enough water (about 1 cup) to make a firm dough, then knead for 4–5 minutes. Place dough in a bowl and set aside for 30 minutes.

Divide the dough into 16 golfball-sized balls, flatten into discs with your hands, dust with a little extra flour, then roll out to 12-cm (5-in) rounds. Heat a dry, heavy-based frying pan to hot and cook each chapati for 30 seconds, turning once (the underside should be brown-flecked before you turn the chapati).

Keep the cooked chapatis warm while you cook the remainder. Brush with a little melted ghee or butter before serving, if you like.

Atta flour is a wholemeal flour that is finer in texture than Western wholemeal flour. It is available at Indian grocers. Alternatively, use a mix of two-thirds wholemeal flour and one-third plain flour.

Garlic Parathas

Makes 8–10

2 cups (290 g/10 oz) chapati
flour (atta) (see note page 54)

¼ teaspoon salt

1 teaspoon vegetable oil

10 cloves garlic, crushed

1 tablespoon (20 ml/¾ fl oz)
melted ghee

Combine the sifted flour, salt and 1 cup (250 ml/8½ fl oz) water in a bowl. Knead well to form a firm dough. Cover with a damp cloth and set aside for 30 minutes.

Heat the oil in a frying pan over low–medium heat and fry the garlic until golden. Set aside.

Divide the dough into 8–10 small balls. On a lightly floured surface, roll out to rounds about 10 cm (4 in) in diameter. Brush each with a little of the garlic mixture then fold in half and seal the edges. Flatten slightly with your fingers, then roll out to make rounds about 20 cm (8 in) in diameter.

Heat a non-stick frying pan over medium heat. Add a paratha and when underside is half-cooked, turn to cook the other side. Dribble a little ghee on top and then fry both sides over low heat until golden brown. Keep parathas warm while you cook remainder.

Serve hot.

Stuffed Pancakes

Masala dosa

Makes 6–8

vegetable oil for frying

melted ghee, for preparing
dosas

fresh coconut chutney
(page 228), to serve

DOSA BATTER

¾ cup white lentils
(split urad dal)

¾ cup basmati rice

¼ teaspoon fenugreek seeds

½ teaspoon salt

MASALA FILLING

4 large potatoes

1 tablespoon (20 ml/¾ fl oz)
vegetable oil

1 teaspoon black
mustard seeds

¼ teaspoon fenugreek seeds

2 onions, thinly sliced

½ tablespoon crushed garlic

½ tablespoon grated
fresh ginger

¼ teaspoon ground turmeric

1 tomato, chopped

1 teaspoon salt

10 curry leaves

¼ cup chopped fresh
coriander leaves

2 small fresh hot green
chillies, finely chopped

For the batter, soak the lentils in plenty of cold water overnight.

Soak the rice in about 2 cups cold water for 30 minutes. Drain. Place in a
food processor and blend to a thickish paste (the paste should feel a bit
grainy). Transfer to a large bowl. **>**

Drain the lentils, then blend to a paste in the food processor with the fenugreek seeds and the salt. Mix the rice and lentil pastes together, add 1 cup (250 ml/8½ fl oz) water, and stand for 6 hours, or overnight.

Meanwhile, make the masala filling. Boil the potatoes until tender, drain, then peel and mash roughly. Heat the oil in a frying pan and stir-fry the mustard and fenugreek seeds until they start to crackle. Add onions and sauté for 5 minutes. Stir in the remaining filling ingredients, fry for a minute and then set aside.

Check the consistency of the dosa batter: you may need to add a little more water to achieve the right (thickish) pouring consistency.

Prepare dosas one at a time. Heat a non-stick frying pan and brush with a little oil. Pour a large spoonful of batter in the centre, spreading it in a circular motion with the back of the spoon until the surface of the pan is covered. Cook over medium heat until the underside is golden, then spread some ghee in the centre of the dosa and around the sides of the pan. Place 2 tablespoons of the filling in the centre of the pancake, spread gently over the surface, then fold the pancake over.

Sprinkle finished dosa with a little more ghee and serve at once, with fresh coconut chutney.

Puffy Deep-fried Bread

Bhaturas

Makes 10–12

1 cup (150 g/5 oz) plain flour

1 cup (150 g/5 oz) semolina

2 tablespoons (40 ml/1½ fl oz)
  plain yoghurt

1 teaspoon vegetable oil

½ teaspoon salt

oil for deep-frying

Mix together the sifted flour, semolina, yoghurt, vegetable oil and salt, and
bind to a soft dough with a little water. Cover with cling wrap and set aside
in a warm place for 5–6 hours until dough has risen slightly.

Heat oil in a pan suitable for deep-frying.

Knead dough briefly, then divide into 10–12 portions. Roll into discs about
12 cm (5 in) in diameter and deep-fry one at a time in the hot oil, turning
once or twice until golden-brown on both sides. After first turning, press
centre of bhatura with a spoon, which will cause it to puff out. Drain on
paper towels and serve immediately.

⁓ Bhaturas are often served with chickpea or lentil dishes and used to
scoop up the sauce.

Spicy Potato Bread

Aloo paratha

Serves 6–8

- 2 cups (290 g/10 oz) chapati flour (atta) (see note page 54)
- 1¼ teaspoons salt
- 4 potatoes
- ½ teaspoon ground chilli
- ½ teaspoon garam masala
- 1 teaspoon amchur (mango powder)
- 2 tablespoons chopped fresh coriander
- ghee for frying

Place the sifted flour, ¼ teaspoon salt and 1 cup (250 ml/8½ fl oz) water in a bowl, mix, and knead well to form a firm dough. Cover with a damp tea towel and set aside. Boil the potatoes until tender, then mash and combine with the spices, amchur, fresh coriander and 1 teaspoon salt.

Divide the dough into 8–10 golfball-sized balls, then roll out into rounds about 10 cm (4 in) in diameter. Place a round in the palm of your hand, shape into a bowl and spoon about 1½ tablespoons of the potato mixture into the centre. Fold dough to enclose filling and press edges together to seal. Roll out, using a little extra flour, to form a disc about 15 cm (6 in) in diameter. Repeat with the remaining mixture.

Heat a non-stick griddle pan with a little ghee and cook the parathas one at a time. Cook on one side until half-done, turn over, dribble some ghee on the top side and then cook until golden brown on both sides. Serve hot.

Pooris

Puris

Makes about 15

2 cups (290 g/10 oz) chapati
   flour (atta) (see note page 54)

¼ teaspoon salt

2 teaspoons oil

vegetable oil for deep-frying

Place the sifted flour, salt and 2 teaspoons oil in a bowl, and mix together. Make a well in the centre and gradually pour in enough water (about 1 cup) to make a fairly soft dough. Knead for 4–5 minutes, until dough is soft but not sticky. Cover with a damp tea towel and set aside for 20–30 minutes.

Knead dough again, and divide into about 15 golfball-sized balls. Apply a little vegetable oil to each portion and roll out into 7.5-cm (3-in) rounds.

Heat oil over medium heat in a wok or other pan suitable for deep-frying. Deep-fry pooris one at a time, turning once with a slotted spoon and then carefully splashing the top with a little of the hot oil. They will be puffed and golden brown when ready.

Vegetable Dishes

Unsurprisingly for a largely vegetarian nation, Indian cuisine includes myriad delicious dishes using everyday and seasonal vegetables. A basic salad of tomatoes, cucumber and a few chillies is usually offered at a meal, though salads are never a feature.

Most households rely on legumes (dried beans, peas and lentils) to meet their daily protein needs (see Lentils and Other Legumes). Yoghurt, paneer cheese and eggs also provide high levels of protein and calcium, and add interest and texture to vegetable dishes.

Paneer is extremely versatile and can be grilled, fried or added to curries – it retains its shape and size, and doesn't melt. It is easy to make your own paneer (see instructions on page 15).

‹ Quick Spicy Vegetables (page 64)

Quick Spicy Vegetables

Serves 4

½ cup unsalted peanuts

2 tablespoons (40 ml/1½ fl oz) vegetable oil

2 potatoes, peeled and chopped

1 onion, chopped

2 carrots, diced

1 cup fresh or frozen peas

1 cup small cauliflower florets

1 green capsicum, chopped

1 teaspoon salt

1½ teaspoons mild curry powder (page 242) (or Madras curry powder)

½ cup (125 ml/4 fl oz) plain yoghurt, lightly whisked

½ cup (125 ml/4 fl oz) tomato purée

Grind peanuts to a powder in a small grinder and set aside. Heat half the oil in a pan and fry the potatoes until golden brown, then set aside.

Heat the remaining oil in a wok or frying pan and stir-fry the onion until soft (about 5 minutes). Add the carrots, peas, cauliflower and capsicum, and stir-fry until vegetables are just tender, then add the fried potatoes. Add the salt and curry powder, and mix well.

Add yoghurt to the pan, stir in, then add the tomato purée and ground peanuts and stir well. Cook, uncovered, for 5 minutes or until sauce thickens.

Serve hot.

Green Beans with Fenugreek

Serves 4

2 handfuls green beans

2 tablespoons (40 ml/1½ fl oz)
   melted ghee or butter

juice of 1 lime

¼ cup chopped fresh
   coriander leaves

1½ teaspoons fenugreek seeds

salt

Cook the beans in boiling water for 5 minutes, then drain and refresh in cold water.

Heat the ghee or butter in a saucepan over medium heat and stir in the lime juice, coriander and fenugreek. Add the beans and stir to coat. Add salt to taste, and serve hot.

Coconut Mushrooms

Serves 4

1 tablespoon (20 ml/¾ fl oz)
   peanut oil

2 cloves garlic, finely chopped

2 fresh long red chillies, sliced

1 onion, finely chopped

3 cups small button
   mushrooms

⅔ cup (160 ml/5 fl oz)
   coconut milk

salt and freshly ground
   black pepper

¼ cup chopped fresh
   coriander, for garnish

Heat the oil in a heavy-based saucepan and quickly stir-fry the garlic and chillies for 30 seconds. Add the onion and cook until soft and golden. Add the whole mushrooms and stir-fry for another 3 minutes.

Add coconut milk to the pan and bring to the boil. Simmer, uncovered, for 4–5 minutes until the liquid has reduced. Season to taste with salt and pepper.

Garnish with the coriander leaves and serve immediately.

꒰ This dish goes particularly well with fish curries.

꒰ To make spiced button mushrooms, cook mushrooms in a little oil until soft, then add a tablespoon of tomato paste and ½ cup fresh coriander leaves, and cook for a couple more minutes. Serve hot, sprinkled with garam masala.

Indian-style Coleslaw

Serves 4

1 cup shredded cabbage

1 cup thinly sliced celery

1 cup thinly sliced carrot

1 cup thinly sliced bulb fennel

2 spring onions, thinly sliced,
plus extra for garnish

⅓ cup sultanas

½ teaspoon caraway seeds

¼ cup fresh coriander leaves,
plus extra for garnish

1 tablespoon chopped
fresh parsley

3 tablespoons (60 ml/2 fl oz)
olive oil

1 teaspoon freshly squeezed
lemon juice

Place the sliced vegetables in a bowl, add the sultanas and caraway seeds, and toss together lightly. Add the chopped coriander and parsley, the oil and lemon juice, and mix thoroughly.

Chill the salad for 2 hours before serving. Garnish with extra spring onions and coriander.

Madras-style Eggplant

Serves 4

2 teaspoons salt

1 large eggplant, cubed

1 tablespoon (20 ml/¾ fl oz) vegetable oil

1 onion, thinly sliced

1 teaspoon black mustard seeds

4 cloves garlic, thinly sliced

1 large tomato, chopped

1 teaspoon ground chilli

¼ teaspoon ground turmeric

fresh coriander leaves, for garnish

cucumber raita (page 227) and chapatis (page 54), to serve

Dissolve salt in a large bowl of water and soak the eggplant cubes for about 10 minutes. Drain and pat dry.

Heat the oil in a heavy-based frying pan and fry the onion until it is soft and golden. Add the mustard seeds and garlic, cook for another minute, then stir in the tomato, chilli, turmeric and drained eggplant. Cover and simmer for 10 minutes or until the eggplant is cooked.

Garnish with coriander leaves, and serve with raita and chapatis on the side.

Potato with Peas

Aloo mattar

Serves 4

2 tablespoons (40 ml/1½ fl oz) vegetable oil

½ teaspoon cumin seeds

1 small fresh hot green chilli

2.5-cm (1-in) piece fresh ginger, grated

2 cloves garlic, finely chopped

2 large potatoes, peeled and cut into 2.5-cm (1-in) cubes

1 cup (250 ml/8½ fl oz) canned crushed tomatoes

2 teaspoons ground coriander

1 teaspoon ground cumin

¼ teaspoon ground turmeric

salt and freshly ground black pepper

¾ cup fresh or frozen peas

1 teaspoon sugar

chopped fresh coriander leaves, for garnish

Indian bread and hot lime pickle (page 236), to serve

Heat the oil in a frying pan and fry the cumin seeds until they start to pop. Add the whole chilli, ginger and garlic, cook for a few minutes and then add the potatoes. Add ½ cup (125 ml/4 fl oz) water, plus the tomatoes, spices, salt and pepper, cover and bring to the boil. Reduce heat and simmer for 2 minutes, then uncover and simmer until potatoes are almost cooked and sauce reduced. Add peas and sugar, and cook for a few minutes until peas are soft.

Check seasoning and adjust if needed. Serve hot, garnished with fresh coriander and accompanied by pooris or chapatis and hot lime pickle.

Masala Zucchini

Serves 4–6

1 tablespoon (20 ml/¾ fl oz)
  vegetable oil

1 onion, thinly sliced

3 cloves garlic, crushed

2.5-cm (1-in) piece fresh
  ginger, grated

1 × 400-g (14-oz) can crushed
  tomatoes

½ teaspoon ground chilli

4 zucchini, sliced into
  1-cm (⅜ in) rounds

salt and freshly ground
  black pepper

Heat the oil in a heavy-based saucepan and fry the onion, garlic and ginger until soft. Add the tomatoes and chilli, bring to the boil and then simmer, uncovered, for 20 minutes, until the sauce thickens. Add the zucchini and cook for about 5 minutes, until tender. Add salt and pepper to taste.

Paneer with Spinach

Saag paneer

Serves 4

500 g (1 lb 2 oz) fresh
  or frozen spinach

300 g (10½ oz) paneer cheese

3 tablespoons (60 ml/2 fl oz)
  melted ghee

2 cloves garlic, crushed

1 teaspoon garam masala

½ teaspoon freshly
  grated nutmeg

⅓ cup (80 ml/3 fl oz)
  plain yoghurt

salt and freshly ground
  black pepper

If using fresh spinach, place in a saucepan with ½ cup (125 ml/4 fl oz) water and cook, tightly covered, for 4 minutes. Drain, and squeeze out any excess moisture. (Defrost frozen spinach, if using.)

Cut the paneer into bite-sized cubes. Heat the ghee in a large heavy-based pan and fry paneer for 1 minute, turning constantly. Add the garlic, garam masala and nutmeg, and fry for 30 seconds. Pour in the yoghurt, reduce heat and simmer for a few minutes. Stir in the spinach, add salt and pepper to taste, and simmer gently for 3 minutes.

Serve hot.

Cucumber Curry

Serves 4–6 as a side dish

½ cup (125 ml/4 fl oz)
  coconut cream

1 teaspoon sugar

¼ teaspoon ground turmeric

1 red capsicum, chopped

1 large cucumber, cubed

½ cup crushed salted peanuts

2 tablespoons (40 ml/1½ fl oz)
  melted ghee or vegetable oil

1 teaspoon cumin seeds

1 teaspoon black
  mustard seeds

2 dried red chillies, crumbled

4 curry leaves

3 cloves garlic, crushed

whole peanuts, for garnish

Bring ½ cup (125 ml/4 fl oz) water to the boil in a large pan, then add the coconut cream, sugar and turmeric. Lower the heat and simmer, uncovered, for 10 minutes or until sauce has reduced a little. Add capsicum, cucumber and crushed peanuts, and simmer for another 5 minutes. Remove from the heat.

Heat the oil or ghee in a small pan and fry the cumin and mustard seeds until they start to crackle. Add the chillies and cook for a few minutes, making sure the spices don't burn. Reduce heat, add curry leaves and garlic, and fry for 2 minutes. Pour the hot spiced oil over the curry and stir in.

Garnish with whole peanuts and serve warm with fish and chicken curries.

Pumpkin Curry

Serves 6–8

⅓ cup (60 ml/2 fl oz) melted
  ghee or vegetable oil

3 cups diced pumpkin

1½ teaspoons ground cumin

1½ teaspoons ground chilli

¼ teaspoon ground turmeric

1½ cups (375 ml/12½ fl oz)
  coconut milk

salt and freshly ground
  black pepper

3 teaspoons black
  mustard seeds

10 curry leaves

3 small fresh hot
  green chillies

Heat all but 1 tablespoon of the ghee or oil in a large saucepan. Fry the pumpkin with the cumin, ground chilli and turmeric for 1 minute. Add the coconut milk, salt and pepper, cover and simmer for 10 minutes, or until pumpkin is tender and the liquid absorbed.

In a small frying pan, heat the remaining ghee and stir-fry the mustard seeds, curry leaves and whole green chillies for a few minutes until fragrant.

Place the pumpkin in a serving dish and pour the spiced ghee over. Serve the curry warm.

Spicy Eggs

Serves 4

1 tablespoon (20 ml/¾ fl oz) vegetable oil

1 teaspoon grated fresh ginger

1 teaspoon crushed garlic

2 onions, finely chopped

½ teaspoon ground chilli

¼ teaspoon ground turmeric

1 tomato, chopped

1 teaspoon salt

4–6 eggs, soft-boiled and carefully shelled

¼ cup chopped fresh coriander, plus extra for garnish

1 small fresh hot green chilli

naan (page 53), to serve

Heat the oil in a heavy-based saucepan and quickly stir-fry the ginger and garlic. Add the onions, ground chilli and turmeric, and cook for a few minutes until soft. Add the tomato, salt and ½ cup (125 ml/4 fl oz) water to the pan and cook (with lid on) over low heat for 5–7 minutes.

Add the whole eggs, fresh coriander and whole chilli to the pan, turn the heat up for a few seconds and gently stir to warm the eggs.

Garnish with a little extra coriander and serve warm with naan bread.

Spicy Potato & Cauliflower

Serves 4

2 tablespoons (40 ml/1½ fl oz)
  vegetable oil

1 teaspoon cumin seeds

1 onion, finely sliced

2 large potatoes, peeled and
  cut into chunks

1 medium-sized cauliflower,
  separated into florets

3 cloves garlic,
  roughly chopped

2.5-cm (1-in) piece fresh
  ginger, roughly chopped

½ teaspoon ground chilli

½ teaspoon ground coriander

½ teaspoon ground turmeric

2 tomatoes, chopped

Heat the oil in a frying pan and gently fry the cumin seeds until they begin to crackle. Add the onion and sauté until soft and golden brown.

Add the potato and cauliflower to the pan and fry gently for 5 minutes. Remove this mixture from the pan and set aside.

Pound or process the garlic and ginger to a paste. Add to the still-warm pan and fry for a few minutes. Add the ground spices and the tomatoes, and fry for a few minutes. Return potato and cauliflower to the pan and cook over low heat for 10 minutes, until the potato is soft. Serve hot.

This is quite a dry curry, but you can add some water if you prefer a little more moisture.

Dry Curry of Potatoes

Sukhe aloo

Serves 4–6

4–5 medium-sized potatoes

2 tablespoons (40 ml/1½ fl oz)
vegetable oil

4 curry leaves

¾ teaspoon black
mustard seeds

2 dried red chillies, crumbled

½ teaspoon ground turmeric

¾ teaspoon salt

chopped fresh coriander
leaves, for garnish

Boil the potatoes until cooked then peel, dice and set aside to cool.

Heat the oil in a heavy-based pan over medium heat. Add the curry leaves, mustard seeds, chillies and turmeric, and stir-fry for a few moments.

Add the potatoes and salt to the pan, and cook for a few minutes until potatoes are heated through. Garnish with chopped coriander and serve at once.

Quick Paneer Scramble

Serves 4

1 tablespoon (20 ml/¾ fl oz)
vegetable oil

1 onion, chopped

1 teaspoon grated
fresh ginger

1 tomato, chopped

½ green capsicum,
finely chopped

500 g (1 lb 2 oz) paneer
cheese, crumbled

salt

toast, to serve

Heat the oil in a frying pan and fry the onion and ginger until softened. Add the tomato and capsicum, and cook for a few minutes until tomato is soft.

Add the paneer to the pan and stir for 2 minutes, until heated through. Add salt to taste, and serve on toast for breakfast or a light lunch.

Mushrooms with Peas

Serves 4

⅓ cup (80 ml/3 fl oz)
  vegetable oil

2 onions, finely chopped

2 teaspoons crushed garlic

2 teaspoons grated
  fresh ginger

1 small fresh hot green chilli

3 cups button mushrooms,
  halved

6 tomatoes, chopped

2 cups fresh peas

½ teaspoon ground turmeric

1 teaspoon ground coriander

½ teaspoon ground chilli

½ cup fresh coriander leaves

5 curry leaves

salt

Heat the vegetable oil in a large heavy-based saucepan and sauté the onion for 5 minutes, until soft and golden brown. Add the garlic and ginger, stir, cook for 2 minutes and then add the whole fresh chilli and cook for another minute.

Add the mushrooms to the pan and cook for a few minutes, until they soften slightly. Next add the chopped tomatoes and cook for 2 minutes. Add the peas, cover the pan and simmer over low heat for 10 minutes, stirring occasionally. Increase heat to medium and add the ground spices, along with the coriander and curry leaves. Stir well, then simmer for another 2 minutes or until peas are tender. Check the seasonings before serving, adding salt if necessary.

Spinach & Potato Curry

Serves 4

- 1 tablespoon (20 ml/¾ fl oz) vegetable oil
- 1 teaspoon black mustard seeds
- 1 onion, thinly sliced
- 2 cloves garlic, crushed
- 2.5-cm (1-in) piece fresh ginger, finely chopped
- 4 large potatoes, peeled and cut into chunks
- ½ teaspoon ground chilli
- 1 teaspoon salt
- 2 cups fresh or frozen (defrosted) spinach
- ¼ teaspoon garam masala

Heat the oil in a heavy-based saucepan and fry the mustard seeds until they start to sputter. Add the onion, garlic and ginger, and fry for 5 minutes, stirring, until the onions are soft and golden.

Add the potatoes, chilli, salt and 3 tablespoons (60 ml/2 fl oz) water, and fry for a further 5 minutes. Now add the spinach and garam masala to the pan, cover and simmer for 10–15 minutes until the potatoes are cooked and the spinach has wilted. Adjust the liquid to your preference: add more water, or cook for a few more minutes to reduce the liquid.

Serve hot.

Vegetable Korma

Serves 4

⅔ cup unsalted cashews

4 small new potatoes

⅓ cup (80 ml/3 fl oz)
vegetable oil

1 onion, finely chopped

2 teaspoons crushed fresh
ginger

2 small fresh hot green
chillies, finely chopped

2 teaspoons ground coriander

½ teaspoon ground turmeric

1½ cups (375 ml/12½ fl oz)
vegetable stock

1 small cauliflower,
divided into florets

½ cup sliced green beans

½ cup sliced carrots

½ teaspoon salt

2 tablespoons (40 ml/1½ fl oz)
cream

extra ½ cup toasted cashews,
for garnish

Soak the cashews in ½ cup (125 ml/4 fl oz) hot water for 10 minutes, then drain. Blend to a smooth paste in a food processor. Set aside.

Boil the potatoes in lightly salted water until just tender, then cut each in half and set aside.

Heat the oil in a heavy-based saucepan and cook the onion, ginger and chillies over medium heat for 5 minutes, until the onion is soft. Add the coriander and turmeric, and cook for 1 minute, stirring to ensure the spices don't burn. ❯

Spicy Okra

Serves 4–6

⅓ cup (80 ml/3 fl oz)
vegetable oil

500 g (1 lb 2 oz) okra,
trimmed and cut in
half crossways

5-cm (2-in) piece fresh
ginger, grated

3 large cloves garlic, chopped

1 teaspoon black
mustard seeds

1 large onion, finely chopped

½ teaspoon ground turmeric

½ teaspoon ground chilli

½ teaspoon salt

2 tomatoes, chopped

Heat half the oil in a wok or non-stick frying pan and fry the okra over low heat for about 10 minutes, until they are no longer oozing sticky juice. Remove from heat, place in a bowl and set aside.

Place ginger and garlic in a mortar or processor and blend to a paste. Over high heat, add the remaining oil to the pan. Stir-fry the mustard seeds for a minute, then add the onion and cook for 2 minutes. Add garlic–ginger paste and cook for 2 minutes until onion is lightly browned. Reduce heat, add spices and mix well. Add okra and the salt, stir well to combine and then add the tomatoes. Stir again, cover, and simmer for 5 minutes.

Add 1 tablespoon (20 ml/¾ fl oz) water to the pan, stir well and cook for another 5 minutes. Serve with plain white rice or Indian bread.

Paneer with Peas & Spices

Mattar paneer

Serves 4–6

3 tablespoons (60 ml/2 fl oz) vegetable oil

250 g (9 oz) paneer cheese, cubed

1 onion, finely chopped

2.5-cm (1-in) piece fresh ginger, roughly chopped

4 cloves garlic, crushed

1 small fresh hot green chilli

¼ cup chopped fresh coriander, plus extra for garnish

½ teaspoon ground coriander

1 teaspoon ground cumin

½ teaspoon ground chilli

1 teaspoon salt

3 tomatoes, chopped

1 cup fresh or frozen peas

½ teaspoon garam masala

Heat about 2 tablespoons of oil in a non-stick pan and fry the paneer over low heat for about a minute. Remove from the pan and set aside.

In a grinder or mortar, blend the onion, ginger, garlic, fresh chilli and coriander to a smooth paste with a little water. Add remaining oil to the pan and fry the paste for about 5 minutes. Add the ground spices and salt, fry for 1 minute, then add tomatoes, fresh peas (if using) and 1½ cups (375 ml/ 13½ fl oz) water. Bring to the boil, add the paneer and frozen peas (if using), mix well and simmer for 15 minutes. Check liquid and seasonings, adjust if necessary, and garnish with fresh coriander and garam masala.

Serve with plain rice or Indian bread.

Masala Cabbage

Serves 4

2 tablespoons (40 ml/1½ fl oz) melted ghee or vegetable oil

1 teaspoon cumin seeds

2 small fresh hot green chillies, deseeded and chopped

1 onion, sliced

½ teaspoon asafoetida

2½ cups finely shredded cabbage

2 carrots, grated

¼ teaspoon garam masala, plus extra for garnish

salt

juice of 1 lemon

Heat the ghee or oil in a heavy-based pan and fry the cumin seeds and chillies for about 30 seconds, until the cumin seeds begin to pop and crackle. Add the onion and asafoetida, and cook for another 4 minutes until the onion is soft and golden.

Add the cabbage, carrots and garam masala to the pan and stir-fry for 5 minutes, or until the cabbage is soft. Add salt to taste, sprinkle with extra garam masala and lemon juice, and serve hot.

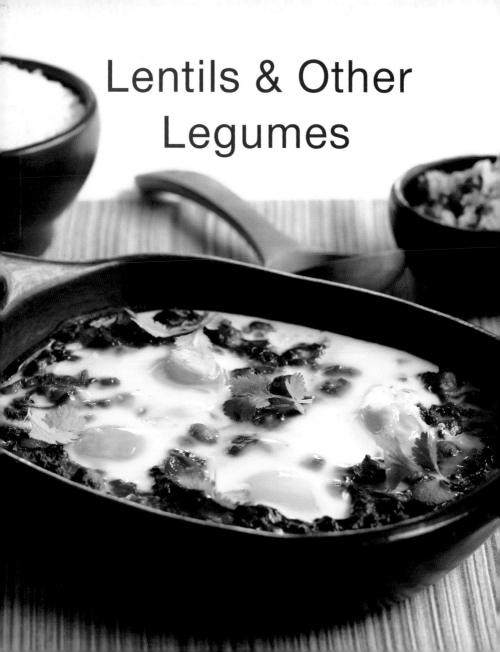

Lentils & Other Legumes

Legumes, such as lentils, chickpeas and red kidney beans, are staples of Indian cooking. They are inexpensive, satisfying and high in protein, fibre and iron.

Some form of dal (a dish of pulses such as lentils or split peas) is usually served at every meal, on it own or cooked with seasonal vegetables. There are thousands of regional takes on basic dal dishes and it is worth experimenting to find your favourite. Usually dal is garnished with spiced oil, called a tarka.

There are many varieties of lentils used in India, with countless colours, flavours and textures available. Some are used whole, while others are bought split. The recipes here use some of the more common lentil varieties: black, red and yellow lentils, and mung beans. (See Special Ingredients, page 246, for more information on the specific lentil types.) Dried lentils can be stored in a cool, dry place for up to a year.

< Balti Chickpea & Spinach Curry with Eggs (page 98)

Balti Chickpea & Spinach Curry with Eggs

Serves 4

1 cup dried chickpeas

2 tablespoons (40 ml/1½ fl oz) vegetable oil

1 teaspoon crushed cumin seeds

2 teaspoons crushed coriander seeds

4 cloves garlic, crushed

1 × 400-g (14-oz) can crushed tomatoes

1 teaspoon tamarind paste, dissolved in ½ cup (125 ml/ 4 fl oz) hot water

1 teaspoon salt

½ teaspoon ground turmeric

2 teaspoons black mustard seeds

¼ teaspoon ground cayenne or paprika

3 cups fresh spinach

4 eggs

roughly chopped fresh coriander leaves, for garnish

Soak the chickpeas in plenty of water overnight. Drain, then cover with fresh water and bring to the boil. Simmer until soft (30–45 minutes). Drain.

Preheat oven to 180°C (360°F).

Heat the oil in a heavy flameproof casserole dish and stir-fry the cumin and coriander seeds for 1 minute. Add the garlic, tomatoes, tamarind water, salt and spices, and stir well.

Add chickpeas to the pan, cover and cook over low heat for 10–15 minutes. Stir in the spinach leaves, cover and simmer for another 4 minutes until the spinach wilts. Remove the lid and if the mixture is fairly wet cook for a few more minutes until the sauce reduces.

Make four wells in the surface of the chickpea mixture and break an egg into each one. Cover, and cook in preheated oven for about 10 minutes, until the eggs are just set. Serve garnished with chopped fresh coriander.

- If you are short of time, use 2 cups canned chickpeas (rinsed and drained) instead of the dried.
- Balti food is essentially a British invention, believed to have originated in the city of Birmingham. Balti dishes are generally easy to make and are subtly spiced, with everything cooked and served in a single pot called a balti. These dishes usually need only a simple accompaniment, such as naan bread.

Fried Potato Patties

Aloo tikki

Serves 4–6

1¼ cups dried whole
  mung beans

1 kg (2 lb 3 oz) potatoes

3 teaspoons cumin seeds

3 tablespoons (60 ml/2 fl oz)
  vegetable oil, plus extra
  for frying patties

2 teaspoons ground turmeric

1 teaspoon ground chilli

1 teaspoon salt

1 teaspoon amchur
  (mango powder)

onion and mint chutney
  (page 230), to serve

Soak the beans in plenty of cold water for 30 minutes. Drain.

Meanwhile, boil potatoes in a saucepan of salted water until tender, then drain, peel and mash.

Toast the cumin seeds in a small pan, then pound or process to a powder and set aside.

Heat the oil in a pan, add the drained beans, the turmeric, ground chilli, prepared cumin, salt and about 1 cup water. Cook over medium heat for 20 minutes, add the amchur and cook for a few more minutes (adding more water if required). Set aside.

Divide mashed potato into about ten fist-sized portions. With greased hands, form each portion into a ball and then flatten into a patty.

Place 2 teaspoons of the bean mixture in the centre of each patty, then press the edges together to seal the filling. Flatten patty again.

Heat a little oil in a frying pan, add the patties in batches and cook over medium heat, turning when underside is crisp. When crisp and golden on both sides, remove patties and drain on paper towels. Keep warm while you cook the remainder.

Serve hot, with onion and mint chutney.

Lentils with Winter Vegetables

Serves 4–6

⅓ cup (80 ml/3 fl oz)
  vegetable oil

½ teaspoon black
  mustard seeds

1 teaspoon cumin seeds

1 dried red chilli, crumbled

8 curry leaves

1 teaspoon crushed garlic

¼ cup desiccated coconut

¾ cup split red lentils
  (masoor dal)

¼ teaspoon asafoetida

½ teaspoon ground turmeric

3 cups chopped mixed
  winter vegetables (carrots,
  cauliflower, green beans,
  peas, zucchini, etc.)

1 tablespoon (20 ml/¾ fl oz)
  tamarind paste

½ teaspoon garam masala

3 tomatoes, quartered

4 cloves garlic, sliced

1 tablespoon (20 ml/¾ fl oz)
  melted ghee

Heat oil in a large saucepan and fry the mustard and cumin seeds, chilli, curry leaves, garlic and coconut for 2 minutes, until the coconut browns.

Mix in the lentils, asafoetida and turmeric, add 2 cups (500 ml/17 fl oz) warm water and stir. Simmer for 20 minutes, uncovered, until the lentils are mushy. Add the mixed vegetables, tamarind paste, garam masala and tomatoes to the pan and cook for a few minutes until the vegetables soften.

In a small pan fry the garlic slices in the ghee until golden. Pour this garnish over the curry just before serving.

Creamy Black Lentils

Dal makhani

Serves 4–6

1 cup whole black lentils (urad dal)

2.5-cm (1-in) piece fresh ginger, chopped

6 cloves garlic

1 teaspoon ground chilli

2 teaspoons salt

1 teaspoon dried fenugreek leaves (kasoori methi)

½ cup (125 ml/4 fl oz) tomato purée

½ cup (125 ml/4 fl oz) cream, plus extra to serve

½ teaspoon garam masala

1 tablespoon (20 ml/¾ fl oz) melted ghee

1 teaspoon cumin seeds

Rinse the lentils, then soak for 20 minutes in cold water. Drain.

Preheat the oven to 130°C (265°F).

Place drained lentils in a heavy-based saucepan with 1.5 L (3 pt 3 fl oz) water, the ginger, garlic, half the ground chilli, and the salt. Bring to the boil, cover pan, and simmer until lentils are soft (about 1 hour).

Meanwhile, dry the fenugreek leaves in the oven for 10 minutes. Remove from heat and crush to a fine powder.

In a separate pan, cook the tomato purée over medium heat for a few minutes, then add the cream, garam masala and crushed fenugreek leaves. Pour this mixture into the dal and simmer for 5–10 minutes.

Heat the ghee in a small saucepan, add the cumin seeds, sizzle quickly and then remove from heat. Add remaining ground chilli and mix well, then add this spicy ghee to the dal and stir well.

Drizzle dal with a little extra cream before serving.

🪷 You can substitute 2–3 large fresh tomatoes, pulsed in a blender, for the tomato purée.

Yellow Lentil Curry

Serves 4–6

1 cup yellow lentils (toor dal)
or split chickpeas (chana dal)

2 tablespoons (40 ml/1½ fl oz)
melted ghee

6 cloves garlic, chopped

4 small fresh hot green
chillies, chopped

½ teaspoon black
mustard seeds

½ teaspoon cumin seeds

½ cup chopped fresh
coriander, plus extra
for garnish

1 teaspoon salt

In a large saucepan cook the lentils in 2 cups (500 ml/17 fl oz) water for 20 minutes (or longer for chana dal), until soft and mushy.

In a separate pan heat the ghee over medium heat and quickly fry the garlic, green chillies, and mustard and cumin seeds. Add the fresh coriander and stir thoroughly, then gradually ladle in the undrained lentils. Add the salt and ½ cup (125 ml/4 fl oz) water, stir well, check the seasonings and turn heat off.

Before serving, check the consistency of the dal and add more water if you prefer a thinner version. Serve warm, garnished with coriander leaves.

Chickpea Curry

Masala chana

Serves 4

1 cup dried chickpeas
(or 2 cups canned chickpeas,
rinsed and drained)

1 tablespoon (20 ml/¾ fl oz)
vegetable oil

2 onions, finely chopped

2 teaspoons crushed garlic

2 teaspoons grated fresh
ginger

2 tomatoes, chopped

1 small fresh hot green chilli,
finely sliced

1 teaspoon chana masala
(page 240)

1 teaspoon salt

¼ teaspoon ground turmeric

½ teaspoon garam masala

¼ cup fresh coriander leaves,
for garnish

If using dried chickpeas, soak overnight in plenty of cold water. Drain, place
in a saucepan with enough fresh water to just cover and bring to the boil.
Reduce heat and simmer until cooked (45–60 minutes). Drain chickpeas,
reserving the cooking water.

Heat the oil in a large saucepan and fry the onions, garlic and ginger. In a
small food processor blend the tomatoes with the green chilli and add this
mixture to the pan along with the chana masala mix, salt and turmeric. Stir
well and cook for a few minutes.

Add the chickpeas with about a cup of the reserved cooking water (or add the canned chickpeas, if using, with about 1 cup water), bring to the boil and simmer for 10 minutes.

Check the consistency of the curry: you can add more water or, if you prefer a thicker sauce, mash a few of the chickpeas with the back of a wooden spoon. Serve hot, garnished with coriander leaves.

Kidney-bean Curry

Serves 4–6

2 tablespoons (40 ml/1½ fl oz) vegetable oil or melted ghee

1 onion, finely chopped

2.5-cm (1-in) piece fresh ginger, grated

4 cloves garlic, crushed

2 teaspoons ground coriander

1 teaspoon ground cumin

½ teaspoon ground chilli

½ teaspoon ground turmeric

2 tomatoes, chopped

1 small fresh hot green chilli, finely sliced

2 cups canned kidney beans, drained

salt

¼ cup chopped fresh coriander leaves, for garnish

½ teaspoon garam masala, for garnish

Heat the oil or ghee in a large heavy-based saucepan and sauté the onion, ginger and garlic until soft and golden. Add the ground spices, fry for a minute, then add the tomatoes and green chilli. Cook for another 2 minutes then add the drained kidney beans.

Stir well, then add 4 cups (34 fl oz) water and bring to the boil. Simmer for 20 minutes, mashing a few of the beans with a wooden spoon to thicken the curry.

Add salt if desired, and serve garnished with chopped coriander and a sprinkle of garam masala.

Mixed Dal

Serves 4–6

1 cup split red lentils
(masoor dal)

1½ cups yellow lentils (toor dal)

2 tablespoons (40 ml/1½ fl oz)
melted ghee or vegetable oil

1½ tablespoons black
mustard seeds

1 tablespoon ground cumin

10 curry leaves

1 onion, diced

2 cloves garlic, crushed

2 teaspoons grated ginger

1 teaspoon ground turmeric

2 teaspoons ground coriander

1 large fresh hot green
chilli, finely chopped

3 tomatoes, chopped

3 cups (750 ml/1½ pt) chicken
or vegetable stock

½ cup (125 ml/4 fl oz)
coconut milk

naan (page 53), to serve

Rinse the lentils, then soak in plenty of water for 30 minutes. Drain.

Heat the ghee or oil in a large saucepan and briefly fry the mustard seeds, cumin and curry leaves. Add the onion, garlic and ginger, and cook, stirring, over medium heat until the onion has softened. Add turmeric, coriander, chilli, tomatoes and lentils, and mix over low heat. Pour in stock, bring to the boil, then cover and simmer for about 1 hour, until lentils are soft.

Just before serving add the coconut milk and return dal briefly to the boil. Serve with naan bread.

Chickpea Dish from North India

Chana kadai

Serves 6

- 1½ cups dried chickpeas
- 1 teaspoon salt
- 2 teaspoons grated fresh ginger
- 2 tablespoons (40 ml/1½ fl oz) vegetable oil
- 1 Indian bay leaf
- 1 black cardamom pod, bruised
- ½ teaspoon cumin seeds
- 1 teaspoon ground chilli
- 2 teaspoons ground coriander
- 1 teaspoon amchur (mango powder)
- ½ teaspoon garam masala

Soak the chickpeas overnight in plenty of cold water. Drain. Place in a large saucepan with 1.5 L (3 pt 3 fl oz) water, salt and half the grated ginger, and simmer until tender (about 1 hour). Set aside.

Heat the oil in a separate large saucepan, add the bay leaf, cardamom, cumin seeds and remaining ginger, and stir-fry for a few seconds. Add the ground chilli and coriander, the amchur and garam masala, stirring thoroughly.

Add the undrained chickpeas to the pan and cook for another 5–10 minutes. Remove the cardamom pod and bay leaf before serving. This dish is good accompanied with Indian bread.

Seafood

Bordered on two sides by sea, India has a vast coastline and its people enjoy a multitude of fish and seafood. The Ganges and other waterways are also important sources of fish for the people living nearby.

Each region uses distinctive flavourings to give seafood dishes their own unique taste. In Bengal, mustard and tomatoes are a feature; Chennai and the south use a lot of coconut milk; and Goa is known for its use of vinegar and tamarind. The kokum tree grows only around the state of Kerala and the region uses this unusual fruit as a souring agent in some seafood curries.

‹ Bengali Salmon (page 116)

Bengali Salmon

Serves 4

4 salmon fillets

½ teaspoon garam masala

1¼ teaspoons salt

juice of 1 lemon

2 tablespoons (40 ml/1½ fl oz) vegetable oil

1 teaspoon black mustard seeds

8 curry leaves

1 onion, finely chopped

2 teaspoons grated fresh ginger

1 teaspoon crushed garlic

1 small fresh hot green chilli, finely chopped

2 × 400-g (14-oz) cans crushed tomatoes

1 tablespoon chopped fresh coriander, plus extra for garnish

1 teaspoon ground coriander

¼ teaspoon ground turmeric

pinch of crushed fenugreek seeds

Sprinkle the salmon pieces with the garam masala and ¼ teaspoon salt, then squeeze the lemon juice over. Set aside.

Heat the oil in a wok or large frying pan, add the mustard seeds and curry leaves and stir-fry for 30 seconds. Add the onion, ginger, garlic and chilli, and fry until the onion is soft and golden-brown.

Add the tomatoes and fresh coriander to the pan, cook for 1 minute, then add 1 teaspoon salt and the spices, and fry for a minute. Pour in ½ cup (125 ml/4 fl oz) water, bring to the boil, reduce heat and then simmer for 5 minutes, until the sauce reduces.

Add the salmon fillets to the sauce and simmer for 8–10 minutes, until the fish is cooked to your liking. Garnish with fresh coriander and serve with plain rice.

Fish Curry from Hyderabad

Serves 8

1 kg (2 lb 3 oz) firm white fish fillets, cut into chunks

1 teaspoon salt

1½ teaspoons ground chilli

3 teaspoons ground coriander

1½ teaspoons ground turmeric

1½ tablespoons grated fresh ginger

6 onions, chopped

1 cup (250 ml/8½ fl oz) vegetable oil

1 cinnamon stick, broken into 3 pieces

10 cloves

2 dried red chillies, crumbled

8 cloves garlic, crushed

1 teaspoon salt

2 × 400-g (13½ fl oz) cans crushed tomatoes (or use 10 fresh tomatoes, chopped)

10 curry leaves

3 small fresh hot green chillies, slit lengthways

½ cup chopped fresh coriander leaves

1 teaspoon garam masala

Place fish in a bowl and add the salt, ½ teaspoon ground chilli, 1 teaspoon ground coriander, 1 teaspoon turmeric and 1 teaspoon fresh ginger. Mix thoroughly and set aside for about 20 minutes.

Purée the onions in a food processor.

Heat the oil in a large saucepan, add the cinnamon, cloves, puréed onions and dried chillies. Cook over medium heat, stirring, until the onions are brown, then add remaining ginger and the garlic and cook for 2 minutes.

Add the remaining turmeric and the salt to the pan, then add the fish and stir in the tomatoes and 2 cups (500 ml/17 fl oz) warm water. Cook (uncovered) over low heat, stirring occasionally, for 10–12 minutes or until the fish is cooked.

Add remaining ground coriander to the pan, along with the curry leaves, green chillies, fresh coriander and garam masala. Cook for 5 minutes, then check the seasonings and adjust if needed. Serve with plain rice.

Chilli-fried Fish

Serves 4

500 g (1 lb 2 oz) firm
white fish fillets

salt

1 teaspoon ground turmeric

5 small dried red chillies,
crumbled

6 cloves garlic, peeled

1 onion, thinly sliced

⅔ cup (160 ml/5 fl oz)
vegetable oil

1 tomato, chopped

1 tablespoon tamarind paste,
dissolved in ½ cup (125 ml/
4 fl oz) warm water

2 teaspoons sugar

2 tablespoons (40 ml/1½ fl oz)
hot chilli sauce

2 tablespoons (40 ml/1½ fl oz)
white vinegar

fresh coriander leaves,
for garnish

Place the fish fillets in a large bowl and season with ½ teaspoon salt and the turmeric. Set aside for about 30 minutes. Soak the chillies in 2 tablespoons (40 ml/1½ fl oz) warm water for 10 minutes. Drain.

Combine the drained chillies with the garlic and onion in a mortar or food processor and grind to a paste.

Heat the vegetable oil in a large frying pan and fry the fish fillets until golden on both sides. Drain on paper towels and set aside. ❯

Add the garlic–chilli paste to the pan with the tomato and fry until tomato softens. Add 1 cup (250 ml/8½ fl oz) water, the tamarind mixture, sugar, a little extra salt and the chilli sauce. Bring to the boil, then lower heat and simmer for 10 minutes until the sauce reduces.

Gently add the fried fish to the pan and stir in the vinegar. Cook for a few minutes until the fish is warmed through. Serve hot, garnished with fresh coriander.

Goan Fish Curry

Serves 4

1 onion, chopped

2.5-cm (1-in) piece fresh
ginger, chopped

3 cloves garlic, chopped

⅓ cup (80 ml/3 fl oz)
vegetable oil

2 teaspoons ground coriander

1 teaspoons ground cumin

1 teaspoon salt

2 tablespoons tamarind paste,
dissolved in ⅔ cup (160 ml/
5½ fl oz) hot water

1 cup (500 ml/17 fl oz)
coconut milk

500 g (1 lb 2 oz) firm white
fish fillets, cut into chunks

½ cup fresh coriander
leaves, for garnish

2 fresh red chillies, deseeded
and finely sliced, for garnish

In a food processor, blend the onion, ginger and garlic to a smooth paste.

Heat the oil in a frying pan over medium heat and fry the onion paste until it
browns. Add the ground coriander, cumin and salt, mix well and then cook
for a few minutes until the oil starts to separate from the mixture. (Add a little
water to the pan if the spices start to stick.)

Pour in the tamarind water and coconut milk, and bring mixture to the boil.
Add the fish and cook over low heat for 10–12 minutes, or until flesh is white
and just cooked. Remove from heat and serve immediately, garnished with
coriander leaves and sliced chillies.

Fish Molee

Serves 4–6

½ teaspoon ground turmeric

1 teaspoon ground chilli

salt and ground black pepper

500 g (1 lb 2 oz) firm white fish fillets, cut into chunks

3 tablespoons (60 ml/2 fl oz) vegetable oil

2 onions, finely chopped

1 teaspoon black mustard seeds

2 teaspoons crushed garlic

2 teaspoons grated fresh ginger

3 small fresh hot green chillies, slit lengthways

10 curry leaves

1½ cups (375 ml/13½ pt) coconut milk

2 tomatoes, chopped

1 tablespoon (20 ml/¾ fl oz) melted ghee

¼ cup chopped cashews

Mix together the turmeric, ground chilli, salt and pepper, and sprinkle over the fish. Set aside for 10 minutes.

Heat oil in a frying pan over medium heat and sauté onions for a few minutes. Add mustard seeds, garlic, ginger, chillies and curry leaves and cook for 2 minutes. Pour in 1 cup (250 ml/8½ fl oz) warm water and bring to the boil. Add fish, cover, and simmer for 10 minutes. Add coconut milk and tomatoes, and cook over low heat until tomato is cooked (around 5 minutes).

In a separate small pan, heat the ghee and fry the cashews until brown. Pour nut mixture over the fish before serving.

Red Fish Curry from Kerala

Meen vevichathu

Serves 6

3 pieces dried kokum

5-cm (2-in) piece fresh
ginger, chopped

3 cloves garlic, chopped

2 tablespoons (40 ml/1½ fl oz)
vegetable oil

2 dried red chillies, crumbled

1 onion, thinly sliced

¼ teaspoon ground turmeric

1 teaspoon salt

500 g (1 lb 2 oz) firm white
fish fillets, chopped

1 teaspoon black
mustard seeds

10 curry leaves

Rinse kokum pieces then soak in 200 ml (7 fl oz) water for 10–15 minutes. Pound or process the ginger and garlic to a paste, then set aside.

Heat half the oil in a pan over low heat and cook the dried chillies for a few minutes until a rich dark colour (add a little warm water if needed, to stop them burning). Add the onion and cook for a few minutes, then add the ginger–garlic paste and cook until soft. Add the kokum and its soaking water, the turmeric, salt, 1 cup (250 ml/8½ fl oz) warm water and fish pieces, and bring to the boil, half-covered. Lower the heat, cover, and simmer for 10 minutes, or until fish is cooked.

In a small saucepan heat the remaining oil over medium heat and fry the mustard seeds and curry leaves. Pour this oil over the fish before serving.

Kerala Prawn Curry

Serves 4

3 pieces dried kokum

2 teaspoons coriander seeds

½ teaspoon ground chilli

6 black peppercorns

¼ teaspoon ground turmeric

3 tablespoons (60 ml/2 fl oz) vegetable oil

1 teaspoon black mustard seeds

1 onion, finely sliced

1 teaspoon grated fresh ginger

8 cloves garlic, crushed

1 small fresh hot green chilli

pinch of fenugreek seeds

10 curry leaves

500 g (1 lb 2 oz) green (raw) prawns, shelled but tails left on

2 cups (500 ml/17 fl oz) coconut milk

salt

Rinse the dried kokum, then soak in ¾ cup (180 ml/6 fl oz) water for about 10 minutes. Meanwhile, grind the coriander, ground chilli, peppercorns and turmeric in a mortar or food processor, and set aside.

Heat the oil in a heavy-based saucepan and fry the mustard seeds until they start to sputter. Add the onion, ginger, garlic and whole green chilli, and cook until onion is soft and golden. Lower the heat and add the ground spice mix plus the fenugreek seeds and curry leaves, and cook, stirring, for another 2 minutes.

Increase heat and add the drained kokum pieces to the pan, along with the soaking water. Cook for a few minutes, until the spices are well mixed, then lower the heat and add the prawns. Cook for 3–4 minutes, then add the coconut milk and simmer for a few minutes until the prawns are cooked.

Discard the kokum and green chilli, add salt to taste, and serve hot with plain rice.

South Indian Prawns

Serves 4

1 tablespoon (20 ml/¾ fl oz) vegetable oil

2 onions, finely chopped

2.5-cm (1-in) piece fresh ginger, grated

3 cloves garlic, crushed

½ teaspoon ground chilli

¼ teaspoon ground turmeric

3 tomatoes, chopped

500 g (1 lb 2 oz) green (raw) prawns, shelled but tails left on

1 teaspoon salt

¼ cup fresh coriander leaves

2 small fresh hot green chillies, deseeded and sliced, for garnish

Heat the oil in a large frying pan and fry the onions, ginger and garlic until soft and golden brown. Stir in the ground chilli and turmeric, then add the chopped tomatoes and cook for 5 minutes, stirring. Add 1 tablespoon (20 ml/¾ fl oz) water to the pan and mix.

Add prawns and salt, and cook until the prawns are pink and firm (about 5 minutes). Add ½ cup (125 ml/4 fl oz) warm water and the coriander leaves and cook for another 5 minutes.

Serve garnished with the green chillies.

Quick Coconut Prawn Curry

Serves 4

2.5-cm (1-in) piece
   fresh ginger, grated

6 cloves garlic, crushed

2 tablespoons (40 ml/1½ fl oz)
   vegetable oil

2 onions, finely chopped

½ teaspoon ground turmeric

1 teaspoon ground chilli

2 tomatoes, chopped

1 teaspoon salt

4 small fresh hot green
   chillies, sliced

500 g (1 lb 2 oz) green (raw)
   prawns, shelled but tails
   left on

400 ml (13½ fl oz)
   coconut milk

juice of 1 lemon

1 cup chopped fresh coriander

In a mortar or food processor, grind the ginger and garlic to a paste. Heat the oil in heavy-based saucepan and fry the onions over medium heat until they start to brown. Add the ginger and garlic paste, and fry for a few minutes. Lower the heat and add the turmeric and ground chilli, and fry for a minute (add a little water if the spices start to stick). Add the tomatoes, salt, fresh chillies and 1 cup (250 ml/8½ fl oz) water. Increase heat, bring to the boil, then add the prawns. Lower the heat, stir in the coconut milk then partially cover and simmer for 8–10 minutes, stirring occasionally.

As soon as the prawns are cooked, squeeze in the lemon juice and remove pan from heat. Stir coriander through and serve curry immediately.

Cochin Mussels

Serves 4–6

3 tablespoons (60 ml/2 fl oz) vegetable oil

1 teaspoon black mustard seeds

1 onion, finely chopped

2 cloves garlic, crushed

2 tablespoons (40 ml/1½ fl oz) white vinegar

4 small fresh red chillies

10 curry leaves

½ teaspoon ground turmeric

½ teaspoon ground chilli

salt

1 cup (250 ml/8½ fl oz) coconut milk

2 kg (4 lb 6 oz) mussels, scrubbed and debearded

Heat the oil in a wok or large frying pan over medium heat. Add the mustard seeds and stir for about a minute, until they start to sputter, then add the onion and garlic, and cook for 4 minutes, stirring constantly, until onion is soft and golden-brown.

Add vinegar to the pan, along with the whole red chillies, curry leaves, turmeric, ground chilli and salt, and mix well. Pour in the coconut milk and bring to the boil, stirring, then reduce the heat to very low. Add the mussels, cover the pan and simmer for 3–4 minutes, until the mussels have opened. (Discard any that remain closed.)

Ladle the mussels into deep bowls and spoon some of the cooking liquid over. Serve with warm Indian bread such as naan.

Crab Curry

Serves 4

2 × 750-g (1 lb 10-oz) crabs

1 onion, finely chopped

1 tablespoon mild curry powder (page 242)

3 teaspoons crushed garlic

2 small fresh hot green chillies, finely chopped

1 teaspoon salt

1 teaspoon ground chilli

2 tablespoons (40 ml/1½ fl oz) vegetable oil

1 teaspoon saffron threads

1 cinnamon stick

10 curry leaves

1 cup (250 ml/8½ fl oz) coconut milk

juice of 1 lemon

To prepare the crabs, crack open the claws and body shell, and remove any blackish and fibrous parts. Wash the meat well and cut body meat into two or four pieces.

In a food processor blend the onion, curry powder, garlic, fresh chillies, salt and ground chilli to a smooth paste. Heat the oil in a large saucepan and fry the spice mixture until soft and browned. Stir in the crab meat and add the saffron, cinnamon and curry leaves.

Add ½ cup (125 ml/4 fl oz) warm water to the pan, bring to the boil and simmer for a few minutes until sauce is slightly reduced, then add the coconut milk and stir well. Simmer until crab is cooked (flesh becomes white), about 15 minutes. Add lemon juice and more salt if needed.

Serve hot with plain rice.

卐 Instead of the mild curry powder, you could use a medium curry powder such as Indian yellow curry powder (Clive of India).

Chicken & Duck

Chicken is a popular meat with Indian cooks, as it is so versatile. It may be stir-fried, slowly braised, grilled tandoori-style, or mixed with rice and vegetables for a grand Mughlai-inspired biryani.

Chicken, like duck, marries beautifully with Indian spices and flavourings. Portions such as skinless breast and thigh fillets are popular choices, as they absorb spices well and cook evenly. Duck is popular in the south of the country and around Kerala, where the waterways attract a lot of bird life.

< Butter Chicken (page 140)

Butter Chicken

Murg makhani

Serves 6–8

⅔ cup (160 ml/5½ fl oz) plain yoghurt

2 teaspoons garam masala

1 teaspoon ground turmeric

½ teaspoon ground chilli

1 teaspoon ground cumin

2 teaspoons grated fresh ginger

2 cloves garlic, crushed

750 g chicken breast or thigh fillets (skin off), cubed

½ cup raw cashews

2 tablespoons (40 ml/1½ fl oz) vegetable oil or melted ghee

2 onions, sliced

3 green cardamom pods, bruised

1 cinnamon stick

1 teaspoon ground paprika

1 × 400-g (14-oz) can crushed tomatoes

2 tablespoons chopped fresh coriander

3 tablespoons (60 ml/2 fl oz) cream

salt

toasted cashews, for garnish

Combine yoghurt, garam masala and ground spices in a bowl with the ginger and garlic. Add the chicken pieces, mix well to coat with the flavourings, and set aside.

Soak the raw cashews in ⅔ cup (160 ml/5½ fl oz) hot water for 10 minutes. Drain, then grind in a food processor with about a tablespoon of water to make a smooth paste. Set aside.

Heat the oil or ghee in a large heavy-based saucepan over medium heat and cook the onions, cardamom and cinnamon for 3–4 minutes until the onion softens. Reduce heat, add chicken pieces and their marinade, plus the paprika, tomatoes and ground cashews. Bring to the boil, then reduce heat and simmer for 15–20 minutes or until the chicken is cooked.

Add the fresh coriander and cream to the pan, with salt to taste, and warm through. Garnish with toasted cashews before serving.

Kashmiri Chicken

Serves 6

½ teaspoon saffron threads

4 green cardamom pods, bruised

½ teaspoon coriander seeds

½ teaspoon cumin seeds

1 cinnamon stick

8 peppercorns

4 cloves

1 tablespoon (20 ml/¾ fl oz) melted ghee

1 onion, finely chopped

1 tablespoon crushed garlic

1 tablespoon grated fresh ginger

1¼ cups (310 ml/10 fl oz) plain yoghurt

8 chicken thigh fillets, sliced into strips

¼ cup ground almonds

¼ cup finely chopped pistachio nuts

¼ cup chopped fresh coriander

¼ cup chopped fresh mint

1 teaspoon salt

toasted flaked almonds, for garnish

Place the saffron threads in 1 tablespoon (20 ml/¾ fl oz) hot water and set aside to soak.

Toast the cardamom pods for a few moments in a small dry pan over low heat, then add the coriander and cumin seeds, cinnamon, peppercorns and cloves, and toast briefly. Pound or process all the whole spices (except the cinnamon stick) to a powder, and set aside. **>**

Heat ghee in a casserole dish, add the onion and cook over medium heat until soft and brown (about 5 minutes). Add the garlic and ginger, and cook for another 2 minutes, stirring, then add the powdered spices and the cinnamon stick. Remove from heat and mix in the yoghurt gradually, stirring well. Return pan to heat and cook for another 2–3 minutes, stirring, until the ghee separates and floats to the surface.

Add chicken to the pan and bring to the boil, stirring constantly, then reduce heat, cover, and simmer for 20 minutes, or until chicken is cooked. Stir in the ground almonds, the pistachios, the saffron and its soaking liquid, the coriander and mint, and the salt. Cover pan and simmer for 5 minutes, until the sauce is thickened.

Garnish with some flaked almonds before serving.

Chicken Jalfrezi

Serves 4–6

3 tablespoons (60 ml/2 fl oz) melted ghee or oil

500 g (1 lb 2 oz) chicken breast fillets, cut into cubes

1 onion, finely chopped

2 teaspoons grated fresh ginger

1 clove garlic, crushed

1 green capsicum, chopped

1 red capsicum, chopped

½ teaspoon ground chilli

1 teaspoon ground cumin

2 teaspoons ground coriander

¼ teaspoon ground turmeric

1 teaspoon salt

1 × 400-g (14-oz) can chopped tomatoes

¼ cup fresh coriander

2 small fresh hot green chillies, deseeded and chopped, for garnish

Heat half the ghee or oil in a large frying pan over medium heat and brown the chicken pieces in batches. Set aside.

Add remaining ghee or oil to the pan and fry the onion until golden brown. Stir in the ginger and garlic, and fry for 2 minutes. Now add the capsicum and fry for a few minutes before stirring in the spices and salt.

Pour in the tomatoes with their juice and ½ cup (125 ml/4 fl oz) warm water. Add the browned chicken pieces, reduce heat and simmer for 10 minutes, uncovered, until the sauce is reduced. Stir in the fresh coriander and serve garnished with the chopped green chillies.

Tandoori Chicken

Serves 4

½ cup (125 ml/4 fl oz) plain yoghurt

6 cloves garlic, crushed

2.5-cm (1-in) piece fresh ginger, grated

2 teaspoons tandoori masala (page 239)

1 teaspoon ground chilli

½ teaspoon ground cumin

¼ teaspoon ground turmeric

½ teaspoon salt

8 chicken drumsticks

1 tablespoon (20 g/¾ oz) butter, melted

lemon wedges, for garnish

Briefly whisk the yoghurt until smooth, then add the garlic, ginger, tandoori masala, ground chilli, cumin, turmeric and salt, and mix well.

Make a few incisions in the chicken drumsticks then place the chicken in the yoghurt mixture and turn to coat, rubbing marinade into the incisions. Set aside for 30 minutes.

Preheat grill or barbecue to hot, or oven to 240°C (475°F).

Grill, barbecue or bake the chicken pieces until cooked (15–20 minutes if grilling or barbecuing, 20–25 minutes if baking), basting occasionally with any leftover marinade and the melted butter, and turning to ensure the chicken is cooked evenly.

Serve hot, with lemon wedges for squeezing.

Chicken Madras

Serves 4

1 tablespoon (20 ml/¾ fl oz)
  vegetable oil

2 onions, finely chopped

2 curry leaves

275 g (10 oz) chicken thigh
  fillets, cut into chunks

2 tomatoes, chopped

3 tablespoons (60 ml/2 fl oz)
  tomato purée

¼ teaspoon ground fenugreek

2 teaspoons ground coriander

½ teaspoon ground chilli

¼ teaspoon ground turmeric

2.5-cm (1-in) piece fresh
  ginger, grated

2 cloves garlic, crushed

juice of 1 lemon

freshly ground black pepper

chopped fresh coriander,
  for garnish

2 fresh red chillies, deseeded
  and chopped, for garnish

In a saucepan, heat the oil and fry the onions and curry leaves until onions are soft and golden. Add the chicken pieces and cook until golden.

Stir in the chopped tomatoes, tomato purée, ground spices, ginger, garlic, lemon juice and 1 cup (250 ml/8½ fl oz) warm water. Stir well, bring to the boil, then reduce heat and simmer for about 10 minutes, stirring, until the chicken is cooked and the sauce reduced.

Serve garnished with chopped fresh coriander and chillies.

Chicken Biryani

Serves 4

2 cups basmati rice

½ cup (125 ml/4 fl oz) vegetable oil

3 onions, thinly sliced

3 green cardamom pods, bruised

2 Indian bay leaves

1 cinnamon stick

3 cloves

1 teaspoon grated fresh ginger

3 cloves garlic, crushed

500 g (1 lb 2 oz) skinless chicken breast fillets, cut into 5-cm (2-in) pieces

½ teaspoon ground turmeric

4 tomatoes, chopped

⅔ cup (160 ml/5 fl oz) plain yoghurt, lightly whisked

1 small fresh hot green chilli, chopped

½ teaspoon ground chilli

juice of 1 lemon

1 teaspoon salt

¼ cup chopped fresh coriander leaves

¼ cup chopped fresh mint leaves

Place rice in a bowl, cover with cold water and leave to stand for 30 minutes. Drain rice, place in a large saucepan and add enough water to just cover. Bring to the boil and simmer for 5–7 minutes then set aside with the lid on.

Heat the oil in a large frying pan and fry the onions, cardamom, bay leaves, cinnamon and cloves until the onions are dark brown and crispy. Remove the spices and onion from the pan with a slotted spoon, and set aside.

Add ginger and garlic to the pan along with the chicken and turmeric, and stir-fry for a few minutes until the chicken begins to brown. Remove pan from the heat, then add the tomatoes, yoghurt, fresh and ground chilli, lemon juice, salt, coriander and mint leaves, plus half the fried onions.

Spread the parboiled rice evenly over the chicken mixture, scatter with the fried spices and the remaining fried onions. Cover, cook for 5 minutes over high heat, then lower heat and simmer for another 5–10 minutes. Check the liquid in the pan, and continue to cook until it has all been absorbed.

Stir the dish carefully, discard the whole spices and serve warm.

Spicy Chicken with Lentils

Serves 4

¼ cup yellow lentils (toor daal)

¼ cup split red lentils (masoor dal)

1 tablespoon (20 ml/¾ fl oz) vegetable oil

2 onions, chopped

1 teaspoon grated fresh ginger

1 teaspoon crushed garlic

1 teaspoon salt

1 teaspoon ground coriander

1 teaspoon ground chilli

½ teaspoon ground turmeric

½ teaspoon garam masala

175 g (6½ oz) chicken breast fillets, cubed

¼ cup chopped fresh coriander

1 small fresh hot green chilli, chopped

juice of 1 lemon

2 tomatoes, chopped

1 tablespoon (20 ml/¾ fl oz) melted ghee

1 teaspoon cumin seeds

3 cloves garlic, peeled

3 curry leaves

Place yellow and red lentils in a large saucepan with 2 cups (500 ml/17 fl oz) cold water and bring to the boil. Cook for 30–45 minutes until the lentils are soft and mushy, then drain and set aside.

Heat the oil in a large frying pan and fry the onions until soft and brown. Add the ginger, garlic, salt and ground spices, and sauté for 1 minute (watch carefully, to avoid burning the spices). Add the chicken pieces and fry for 10–15 minutes, stirring constantly, until the chicken is cooked. **>**

Add the fresh coriander and chilli, lemon juice and ⅔ cup (180 ml/6 fl oz) warm water to the pan, and cook for another 3 minutes. Last, add the cooked lentils and the tomatoes, mix well and cook for 5 minutes, until tomatoes have softened (you may need to add more water if mixture becomes too dry).

In a small saucepan heat the ghee and stir-fry the cumin seeds, garlic cloves and curry leaves for a minute, then pour this mixture over the dish before serving. Serve with plain rice.

Chicken Korma

Serves 4

2 tablespoons (40 ml/1½ fl oz) melted ghee or vegetable oil

500 g (1 lb 2 oz) chicken breast fillets, cut into 2.5-cm (1-in) cubes

1 onion, thinly sliced

2 green cardamom pods, bruised

2 cloves

1 teaspoon crushed garlic

1 teaspoon grated fresh ginger

1 teaspoon ground cumin

¼ teaspoon salt

1½ cups (375 ml/12½ fl oz) cream

¼ cup toasted almonds, for garnish

Heat the ghee or oil in a large heavy-based saucepan and brown the chicken pieces in batches for 8–10 minutes, or until browned. Drain on paper towels and set aside.

Add the onion, cardamom and cloves to the pan and stir-fry for 5 minutes, or until the onion is soft. Add the garlic, ginger, cumin and salt, and cook, stirring, for another 3 minutes. Stir in the cream gradually over low heat, then return chicken pieces to the pan. Cover, and simmer for 5 minutes.

Garnish with toasted almonds and serve with plain rice.

A korma is typically a mild curry made creamy by the addition of cream or yoghurt.

Kerala-style Duck Curry

Serves 4

1 cinnamon stick

2 cloves

2 green cardamom pods

2 teaspoons ground coriander

1 teaspoon ground chilli

¼ teaspoon ground turmeric

1 teaspoon aniseed

1 tablespoon (20 ml/¾ fl oz) vegetable oil

1 onion, thinly sliced

1 teaspoon grated fresh ginger

3 cloves garlic, crushed

2 small fresh hot green chillies, halved lengthways and deseeded

350 g (12 oz) duck breast fillets

1½ teaspoons white vinegar

½ teaspoon salt

1½ cups (375 ml/10 fl oz) coconut milk

2 small potatoes, peeled and cut into cubes

1 tablespoon (20 ml/¾ fl oz) melted ghee

½ teaspoon black mustard seeds

2 curry leaves

Grind the cinnamon stick, cloves and cardamom in a mortar or processor, then combine in a bowl with the coriander, chilli, turmeric and aniseed, and set aside. ❯

Heat the oil in a large heavy-based pan and add the onion, ginger, garlic and green chillies. Fry until onions are soft and brown, then stir in the ground spice mixture and sauté for 4–5 minutes.

Add the duck fillets, vinegar and salt to the pan and stir well. Pour in the coconut milk, bring to the boil, then cover and simmer over low heat for 20 minutes, or until the duck is cooked through. Add the cubed potatoes and cook for another 10 minutes or until the potatoes are soft. If desired, remove duck fillets from the pan and slice thickly, then return to the sauce.

In a small saucepan heat the ghee and stir-fry the mustard seeds and curry leaves for a minute. Pour the spiced ghee over the curry just before serving.

Chicken Mulligatawny

Serves 4

450 g (1 lb) skinless
chicken breast fillets

2 green cardamom pods,
bruised

1 cinnamon stick

2 curry leaves

2 teaspoons ground coriander

1 teaspoon ground cumin

¼ teaspoon ground turmeric

3 cloves garlic, crushed

1 onion, finely chopped

1 cup (250 ml/8½ fl oz)
coconut milk

juice of 1 lemon

CRISP-FRIED ONION

3 tablespoons (60 ml/2 fl oz)
vegetable oil

1 onion, thinly sliced

To make the crisp-fried onion, heat the vegetable oil in a frying pan over medium heat and fry the onion until a deep golden-brown colour (about 5 minutes), making sure it doesn't burn. Drain on paper towels.

Place chicken and 1 cup (250 ml/8½ fl oz) water in a large saucepan and bring to the boil, then cover and simmer gently for 15 minutes or until chicken is cooked. Remove chicken from stock, chop and set aside.

Bring stock back to the boil, add the spices, garlic and chopped onion, and simmer for 15 minutes. Strain stock, then return to pan and add the chicken. Simmer for another 5 minutes, until the chicken is warmed through. Add lemon juice and serve garnished with the crisp-fried onion.

Beef, Lamb & Pork

Although eating beef is prohibited for Hindus, there are many communities in India where beef is eaten and, accordingly, many different recipes reflecting the region of origin. Similarly, pork is forbidden to Muslims but is consumed in some areas, such as Goa in the southwest, where the fiery pork vindaloo is something of a local speciality.

The main red meats eaten in India are mutton, buffalo and goat, with lamb available in the cold northern regions of the country such as Kashmir. The Mughlai style of cooking, which originated in the north, introduced rich dishes where yoghurt, dried fruit and nuts are cooked with meat.

As with all areas of Indian cuisine, the most important element in meat cookery is the blend and quantities of spices used.

< Beef with Onions (page 162)

Beef with Onions

Dopiaza

Serves 6–8

2 tablespoons (40 ml/1½ fl oz)
melted ghee

4 onions, thinly sliced

2 tablespoons (40 ml/1½ fl oz)
vegetable oil

750 g (1 lb 9 oz) boneless
chuck steak, cut into
2.5-cm (1-in) cubes

2 teaspoons cumin seeds

2 teaspoons coriander seeds

2 small fresh hot green
chillies, thinly sliced

4 cloves garlic, crushed

2 teaspoons grated
fresh ginger

2 teaspoons salt

1 teaspoon fenugreek seeds

½ teaspoon ground turmeric

1 teaspoon ground cardamom

1 teaspoon ground chilli

2 tomatoes, chopped

1 cup (250 ml/8½ fl oz)
beef stock

1 teaspoon garam masala,
for garnish

Heat the ghee in a small frying pan, add half the sliced onions and fry for
5 minutes until soft and golden-brown. Set aside.

Heat the vegetable oil in a large heavy-based saucepan over high heat and
brown the beef in batches. Remove from the pan and set aside.

Sprinkle cumin and coriander seeds into the saucepan along with the fresh
chillies and stir-fry for a minute, then add the garlic and ginger. Cook for a
few minutes, then reduce heat, add browned beef and mix well.

Add the remaining sliced onions to the pan, plus the salt, fenugreek, ground spices, tomatoes and beef stock, and bring to the boil. Reduce heat, cover and cook for 1½ hours or until the beef is tender and the sauce thickened.

Just before serving, stir the reserved cooked onions through the dish and cook for a further 10 minutes. Garnish with a sprinkling of garam masala.

⌘ Dopiaza means 'double onion' and refers to the two forms of onion (boiled and fried) used in this dish.

Beef in Mild Coconut Sauce

Serves 4

2 tablespoons vegetable oil

2 tablespoons mild curry paste (page 243)

450 g (1 lb) rump steak, cut into 5-cm (2-in) strips

1 cup (250 ml/8½ fl oz) coconut milk

1 cup (250 ml/8½ fl oz) beef stock

2 tablespoons (40 ml/1½ fl oz) freshly squeezed lemon juice

juice and zest of ½ orange

1 tablespoon (15 g/½ oz) sugar

2 Indian bay leaves

6 small pickling onions, peeled

6 small potatoes, halved

1 cup unsalted roasted peanuts

½ cup sliced green beans

1 red capsicum, thinly sliced

Heat the oil in a large heavy-based pan, add the curry paste and cook over medium heat for 30 seconds, stirring. Add the beef in batches and brown for 10 minutes.

Stir in the coconut milk, stock, lemon juice, orange zest and juice, and the sugar and bring to the boil. Add the bay leaves, onions and potatoes, then simmer uncovered for 5 minutes. Reduce heat, stir in the peanuts, beans and capsicum, and simmer for another 10 minutes, until the potatoes are tender.

Beef Vindaloo

Serves 6–8

1 tablespoon (20 ml/¾ fl oz) vegetable oil

1 kg (2 lb 3 oz) stewing beef, cut into 2.5-cm (1-in) cubes

1 teaspoon finely chopped fresh ginger

3 cloves garlic, crushed

2 teaspoons ground coriander

½ teaspoon ground turmeric

1 quantity vindaloo curry paste (page 245)

1 cup (250 ml/8½ fl oz) beef stock

1 teaspoon salt

Heat the oil in a large frying pan and fry the meat in batches over medium heat for 10 minutes or until lightly browned. Set aside.

Add the ginger and garlic to the pan and fry for 2 minutes. Stir in the coriander and turmeric, and fry for another 2 minutes. Add the curry paste and fry for 5 minutes (you may need to add a little more oil if it starts to stick).

Return the beef to the pan, add the stock and salt, and bring to the boil. Reduce heat, cover, and simmer for 1–1½ hours or until meat is tender.

Serve with plain rice.

Steak & Kidney Curry with Spinach

Serves 4

2 tablespoons (40 ml/1½ fl oz) vegetable oil

1 onion, finely chopped

2.5-cm (1-in) piece fresh ginger, sliced

4 garlic cloves, crushed

¼ teaspoon ground turmeric

1 teaspoon salt

2 tablespoons mild curry paste (page 243)

450 g (1 lb) prepared steak and kidney (see note)

200 g (7 oz) spinach, roughly chopped

3 tablespoons tomato paste

1 tomato, chopped

Heat the oil in a non-stick frying pan and gently fry the onion, ginger and garlic until soft and golden-brown. Lower the heat, stir in the turmeric, salt and curry paste, then add the steak and kidney to the pan and mix well.

Cover pan and cook over medium heat, stirring frequently, for 20 minutes or until the meat is just tender. (Add a little water if necessary.) Add the spinach and tomato paste, mix well and cook, uncovered, until spinach is soft and the sauce has reduced. Add the chopped tomato, increase the heat and cook for another 5–6 minutes.

⊰ You can buy prepared beef steak and kidney from most butchers and supermarkets.

⊰ Frozen spinach (defrosted) can be substituted for fresh.

Beef Madras

Serves 4–6

½ cup desiccated coconut

2 dried red chillies, crumbled

2 teaspoons grated
  fresh ginger

6 cloves garlic, chopped

1 tablespoon ground coriander

1 tablespoon ground cumin

1 teaspoon ground chilli

1 cinnamon stick

4 cloves

½ teaspoon black peppercorns

¾ cup (180 ml/6 fl oz)
  coconut cream

700 g (1 lb 9 oz) stewing beef,
  cut into 2.5-cm (1-in) pieces

3 tablespoons (60 ml/2 fl oz)
  melted ghee

2 onions, finely chopped

4 tomatoes, chopped

1 teaspoon salt

1 cup (250 ml/8½ fl oz)
  beef stock

In the bowl of a food processor, combine the desiccated coconut, dried chillies, ginger, garlic, ground and whole spices, and coconut cream. Blend to a smooth paste. Pour mixture into a bowl, add the beef pieces, stir to coat well, then set aside. Marinate for at least 30 minutes.

Heat the ghee in a heavy-based saucepan, add the onions and cook until softened. Add the meat with its marinade and stir over medium heat for 5 minutes. Add the tomatoes, salt and stock and bring to the boil. Reduce heat, cover, and simmer for 1½ hours or until meat is very tender. Cook uncovered for a further 10 minutes if the sauce needs to be reduced.

Grilled Spiced Lamb Cutlets

Serves 4

1 cup (250 ml/8½ fl oz)
plain yoghurt

2 tablespoons grated
lemon zest

1 tablespoon ground cumin

1 tablespoon ground coriander

½ teaspoon ground chilli

1 teaspoon salt

½ cup chopped fresh coriander

12 lamb cutlets

lime wedges, to serve

Make a marinade by combining the yoghurt with the lemon zest, ground spices, salt and fresh coriander in a large bowl. Stir well, add the cutlets and mix well again. Marinate in the fridge for at least an hour, or overnight.

Preheat grill to medium.

Remove cutlets from marinade and grill for 5–7 minutes on each side, or until cooked to your liking. Serve with lime wedges.

Lamb Tikka

Serves 4–6

3 tablespoons (60 ml/2 fl oz)
plain yoghurt

1 teaspoon crushed garlic

1 teaspoon grated fresh ginger

1 teaspoon ground chilli

¼ teaspoon ground turmeric

2 teaspoons ground coriander

1 teaspoon ground paprika

1 teaspoon ground cumin

1 teaspoon salt

juice of 1 lemon

2 tablespoons (40 ml/1½ fl oz)
vegetable oil

½ cup chopped fresh
coriander, plus extra
for garnish

500 g (1 lb 2 oz) lean lamb,
cut into 2.5-cm (1-in) cubes

cucumber raita (page 227),
to serve

Place all the ingredients, except the lamb, in a bowl and mix well. Add the
lamb, stir, then cover bowl and leave to marinate for an hour.

Preheat grill to medium.

Thread the lamb cubes onto metal skewers. Grill for 8–10 minutes, turning
frequently to ensure lamb cooks evenly.

Remove cooked meat from skewers and garnish with chopped coriander.
Serve hot with cucumber raita.

Lamb with Lentils

Dhansak

Serves 4

300 g (10½ oz) stewing
lamb, cubed

½ cup whole red lentils
(masoor dal)

¼ cup yellow lentils (toor dal)

2 onions, chopped

2 tomatoes, chopped

1 cup cubed eggplant

1 cup chopped pumpkin

1 cup sliced zucchini

1 cup chopped fresh
fenugreek leaves

½ cup chopped fresh
coriander leaves

½ cup chopped fresh
mint leaves

1 cinnamon stick

½ teaspoon ground turmeric

½ teaspoon crushed
fennel seeds

1 teaspoon ground chilli

1 teaspoon salt

1 teaspoon sugar

⅓ cup (80 ml/3 fl oz) vinegar

1 tablespoon (20 ml/¾ fl oz)
melted ghee

1 teaspoon cumin seeds

Rinse the lentils in cold water, then drain.

Place the lentils and all other ingredients, except the vinegar, ghee and cumin seeds, in a heavy-based saucepan. Add 1½ cups (400 ml/13½ fl oz) water and bring to the boil. Reduce heat, cover and simmer until the lentils are soft and the lamb is cooked (about 45 minutes). You may need to add more water. **>**

Mash the vegetables and lentils with a wooden spoon. Add the vinegar and stir well.

Heat the ghee in a separate frying pan and fry the cumin seeds until they start to crackle.

Pour ghee mixture over the curry, stir and simmer for another 5 minutes. Serve hot.

Fresh fenugreek leaves are available from Indian grocers. Dried fenugreek leaves (kasoori methi) can be substituted, but use only ⅓ cup, as the flavour of the dried leaves is far stronger.

Bombay Lamb

Serves 4–6

½ cup (125 ml/4 fl oz)
plain yoghurt

2 teaspoons grated
fresh ginger

2 teaspoons crushed garlic

1 teaspoon ground turmeric

1 teaspoon ground chilli

½ teaspoon garam masala

1 teaspoon salt

1 kg (2 lb 3 oz) lean lamb,
cubed

150 ml (5 fl oz) vegetable oil

2 onions, finely chopped

1 cinnamon stick

2 large tomatoes, chopped

10 black peppercorns, crushed

½ cup (125 ml/4 fl oz)
coconut milk

chapatis (page 54) or naan
(page 53), to serve

Prepare a marinade by mixing together the yoghurt, ginger, garlic, ground spices and salt. Add the lamb, stir well, then set aside for at least 1 hour.

Heat the oil in a heavy-based saucepan and cook the onions until golden. Add the lamb and its marinade plus the cinnamon stick. Cook over low heat, covered, for 15–20 minutes. Add tomatoes and crushed peppercorns to the pan, stir, cover and cook for another 10 minutes. Add the coconut milk and cook for 5 minutes over low heat, stirring.

Adjust seasonings and liquid if necessary. Serve hot with chapatis or naan.

Lamb Koftas

Serves 6

KOFTAS

1 onion, chopped

1 clove garlic, chopped

1 teaspoon grated fresh ginger

½ teaspoon salt

½ teaspoon freshly ground black pepper

¼ teaspoon garam masala

1 tablespoon chopped fresh mint

2 tablespoons chopped fresh coriander, plus extra for garnish

600 g (1 lb 5 oz) lamb mince

1 small fresh hot green chilli, chopped

3 tablespoons (60 ml/2 fl oz) vegetable oil

SPICY SAUCE

1 tablespoon (20 ml/¾ fl oz) vegetable oil

½ teaspoon mustard seeds

½ teaspoon cumin seeds

1 onion, chopped

1 clove garlic, chopped

1 teaspoon grated fresh ginger

½ teaspoon ground cumin

1 teaspoon ground coriander

1 teaspoon salt

½ teaspoon ground chilli

1 tablespoon tomato paste

4 tomatoes, chopped

To make the koftas, combine all the ingredients, except the oil, in a food processor and process until the mixture binds together. With wet hands, shape into golfball-sized balls, then cover and chill for about an hour. **>**

Heat the oil in a non-stick frying pan and fry the koftas in batches, until well browned.

To make the sauce, heat the vegetable oil in a heavy-based pan and fry the mustard and cumin seeds until they sputter. Add the onion, garlic and ginger, and fry for 5 minutes. Stir in the remaining ingredients and simmer for another 5 minutes.

Add the cooked koftas to the sauce and simmer for 10 minutes or until koftas are warmed through. Serve garnished with extra chopped coriander.

Lamb, Potato & Spinach Curry

Serves 4

2 tablespoons (40 ml/1½ fl oz) vegetable oil

2 onions, chopped

2 cloves garlic, finely chopped

2 small fresh hot green chillies

2 dried red chillies, crumbled

450 g (1 lb) lean lamb fillets (or boneless lamb leg), cubed

2 teaspoons ground coriander

1 teaspoon ground cumin

1 teaspoon ground cardamom

½ cup (125 ml/4 fl oz) vegetable stock

½ cup (125 ml/4 fl oz) coconut milk

450 g (1 lb) chat potatoes

½ teaspoon garam masala

1½ cups spinach, roughly chopped

salt and freshly ground black pepper

Heat the oil in a large saucepan and fry the onions until soft. Add the garlic, whole fresh chillies and crumbled dried chillies, and cook for a few minutes. Add the meat and ground spices, and cook, stirring frequently, until browned. Pour in stock and coconut milk, bring to the boil, cover, then simmer gently for 20 minutes, until the liquid has reduced. Add the potatoes and garam masala, stir well and simmer uncovered for 15 minutes or until potatoes are tender.

Add spinach, salt and pepper, and cook for a few minutes until spinach has wilted and sauce reduced. Serve immediately with rice or Indian bread.

Minced Lamb with Peas

Keema mattar

Serves 4

2 cloves garlic, chopped

2 teaspoons chopped fresh
ginger

3 tablespoons (60 ml/2 fl oz)
melted ghee or vegetable oil

1 teaspoon cumin seeds

1 small fresh hot green chilli,
finely sliced

8 black peppercorns, crushed

3 cloves

1 onion, finely chopped

400 g (14 oz) lamb mince

1 teaspoon ground turmeric

½ teaspoon garam masala

1 cup (250 ml/8½ fl oz) canned
crushed tomatoes

1 cup fresh or frozen peas

1 teaspoon salt

juice of 1 lemon

1 tablespoon chopped fresh
mint

chapatis (page 54) and
cucumber raita (page 227),
to serve

Place garlic and ginger in a food processor and blend to a smooth paste.

Heat the ghee or oil in a heavy-based saucepan over medium heat. Add the
cumin seeds, stir-fry for a few moments until they crackle, then remove from
heat and stir in the sliced chilli, peppercorns and cloves. Add the onion,
return pan to heat and cook until onion is soft and golden (5–10 minutes).

Add the ginger–garlic paste and lamb mince to the pan, and stir over high
heat until meat is browned. Add the turmeric, garam masala and tomatoes,
and cook over low heat for 10 minutes. >

Add the peas and ½ cup (125 ml/4 fl oz) water to the pan, and simmer until peas are tender (about 10 minutes for fresh peas or 4 minutes for frozen). If the mixture is too liquidy, increase heat until the sauce reduces.

Just before serving, add the salt and lemon juice, and stir in the fresh mint. Serve with chapatis and raita.

Lamb Korma

Serves 4–6

2 tablespoons (40 ml/1½ fl oz) melted ghee

2 onions, thinly sliced

750 g (1 lb 10 oz) boneless stewing lamb, cubed

4 cloves garlic, crushed

2 teaspoons grated fresh ginger

1 cup (250 ml/8½ fl oz) plain yoghurt, lightly whisked

1 teaspoon salt

2 cloves

3 green cardamom pods, bruised

4 black peppercorns

1½ teaspoons ground coriander

2 tablespoons (40 ml/1½ fl oz) thickened cream

2 tablespoons flaked almonds, for garnish

chapatis (page 54), to serve

Heat the ghee in a large non-stick frying pan and cook the onions until golden (5–10 minutes). Remove from the pan and set aside.

In the same oil, lightly brown the lamb in batches, then set aside. Fry the garlic and ginger over medium heat for 2–3 minutes, then return cooked onions and lamb to the pan. Add the yoghurt and cook gently, stirring frequently, until most of the liquid has boiled away. Add ½ cup (125 ml/4 fl oz) water, the salt, cloves, cardamom, peppercorns and coriander, then cover and simmer for 45–60 minutes, or until lamb is tender.

Stir in cream and garnish with almonds. Serve warm with chapatis.

Lamb with Spinach

Saag gosht

Serves 6

2 tablespoons (40 ml/1½ fl oz) melted ghee or vegetable oil

700 g (1 lb 9 oz) lean lamb, cubed

1 small fresh hot green chilli

1 teaspoon crushed garlic

1 teaspoon grated fresh ginger

1 teaspoon salt

1½ teaspoons ground coriander

2 cardamom pods, bruised

1 Indian bay leaf

1 cinnamon stick

400 g (14 oz) spinach, roughly chopped

¾ cup (180 ml/6 fl oz) plain yoghurt

½ teaspoon freshly grated nutmeg

chopped fresh coriander, for garnish

Heat the ghee or oil in a heavy-based saucepan and brown the lamb in batches. Remove and set aside. Add the whole chilli, garlic and ginger to the pan, and cook for 30 seconds. Stir in the browned lamb, salt, coriander, cardamom, bay leaf and cinnamon stick. Pour in 1 cup (250 ml/8½ fl oz) water and simmer for 45 minutes or until the lamb is tender.

Add the spinach, yoghurt and nutmeg to the pan and simmer gently until the spinach has wilted. If there is too much liquid, cook over medium heat until the sauce has reduced. Serve garnished with fresh coriander and accompanied with plain rice.

Lamb with Spices & Apricots

Serves 4

½ cup dried apricots

1 tablespoon (20 ml/¾ fl oz) vegetable oil

1 cinnamon stick

2 green cardamom pods, bruised

1 onion, chopped

½ tablespoon mild curry paste (page 243)

1 teaspoon ground cumin

1 teaspoon ground coriander

1 teaspoon salt

1 cup (250 ml/8½ fl oz) beef stock

500 g boneless stewing lamb (1 lb 2 oz), cut into 2.5-cm (1-in) cubes

crisp-fried onion (page 159), for garnish

Soak the apricots in hot water for 30 minutes. Drain and set aside.

Heat vegetable oil in a large heavy-based saucepan, add the cinnamon stick and cardamom pods, and fry for 2 minutes. Add the onion and cook for 5 minutes over medium heat, until onion is soft.

Add the curry paste to the pan and fry for a few minutes, then stir in the cumin, coriander and salt, and cook for another 2 minutes. Add the drained apricots, the stock and the lamb, bring to the boil, then reduce heat, cover pan and cook for 1 hour, or until the lamb is tender.

Garnish with the crisp-fried onion.

Rogan Josh

Serves 6

3 tablespoons (60 ml/2 fl oz) vegetable oil or melted ghee

750 g (1 lb 10 oz) boneless stewing lamb, cubed

1 teaspoon cumin seeds

4 green cardamom pods, bruised

2 Indian bay leaves

1 onion, finely chopped

3 cloves garlic, crushed

1 tablespoon grated ginger

1 teaspoon ground chilli

1 small fresh hot green chilli, deseeded and chopped

2 teaspoons ground coriander

1 tablespoon tomato paste

½ cup (125 ml/4 fl oz) plain yoghurt

fresh coriander leaves, for garnish

Heat the oil or ghee in a heavy-based saucepan and brown the lamb in batches. Remove with a slotted spoon and set aside on a plate.

Fry the cumin seeds in the same pan until they start to crackle, then add the cardamom and bay leaves, and cook for 2 minutes, stirring continuously. Add the onion, garlic and ginger, and fry for 5 minutes. Stir in the ground and fresh chilli, ground coriander and tomato paste, and cook for 2 minutes. Return the lamb to the pan (with its juices) and cook for another 5 minutes.

Stir in the yoghurt. Add enough water to cover the meat, bring to the boil and simmer, uncovered, for 1 hour or until meat is tender. Garnish with fresh coriander leaves and serve with plain white rice.

Spicy Goat Curry

Raarha gosht

Serves 4

⅔ cup (180 ml/6 fl oz)
vegetable oil

3 onions, thinly sliced

1 tablespoon crushed garlic

4 large tomatoes, diced

½ teaspoon ground turmeric

1 teaspoon ground chilli

2 tablespoons ground
coriander

1 teaspoon salt

500 g (1 lb 2 oz) goat meat
(leg and neck chops)

½ teaspoon crushed
fennel seeds

½ cup (125 ml/4 fl oz) plain
yoghurt, lightly whisked

¼ teaspoon freshly ground
black pepper

Heat the oil in a heavy-based pan and fry the onions over medium heat for about 10 minutes, until they are a deep dark-brown colour. (Stir continuously to ensure the onions cook evenly and don't burn.)

Mix the crushed garlic with 3 tablespoons (60 ml/2 fl oz) water, add to the onions and cook for 2 minutes. Add the tomatoes, ground spices and salt, and cook for 10 minutes over medium heat, until the oil starts to separate from the spices.

Add the meat to the pan and mix well so that the chops are coated with the spices. Cook over medium heat for 10 minutes, then add 3 cups (750 ml/ 1½ pt) boiling water, stir, and reduce heat. Cover and simmer until the meat is very tender (about 45 minutes).

Add the crushed fennel seeds, the yoghurt and pepper to the pan, cover again, and simmer for another 10 minutes. Taste for seasoning and adjust if necessary. Serve with plain rice or chapatis.

꒐ Goat meat is available from specialist meat suppliers. Instead of goat, you can use lamb chump or mid-loin chops.

Spicy Lamb Roast

Serves 6–8

1 teaspoon cumin seeds

1 cinnamon stick

1 green cardamom pod, bruised

6 black peppercorns

3 cloves

½ cup (125 ml/4 fl oz) plain yoghurt

2 teaspoons finely chopped fresh ginger

2 teaspoons crushed garlic

1 small fresh hot green chilli, finely chopped

1 tablespoon chopped fresh coriander

1 teaspoon ground chilli

½ teaspoon garam masala

1 tablespoon (20 ml/¾ fl oz) freshly squeezed lemon juice

2 tablespoons (40 ml/1½ fl oz) vegetable oil

1 × 1.5 kg (3 lb 5 oz) leg of lamb

Toast the cumin seeds, cinnamon stick, cardamom, peppercorns and cloves in a small pan, then grind to a coarse powder in a spice grinder. Place ground spices in a bowl and mix in all the remaining ingredients, except the lamb.

Place lamb leg in a large dish, pour marinade over, turn to coat well, then leave to marinate for 6 hours or overnight in the fridge.

Preheat the oven to 180°C.

Let the lamb return to room temperature before cooking. Put lamb in a roasting dish, cover with aluminium foil and place on centre shelf of preheated oven. Cook for 1 hour 15 minutes before checking meat for doneness. Remove foil for the last 15 minutes of the cooking time, and rest the lamb for 10 minutes before carving.

Reduce the pan juices while the meat is resting, and serve with the lamb.

Kerala Spicy Pork Curry

Serves 4

10 dried red chillies, crumbled

½ tablespoon black peppercorns

1 tablespoon coriander seeds

½ tablespoon cumin seeds

500 g (1 lb 2 oz) pork fillet, chopped into 2.5-cm (1-in) cubes

2 onions, finely chopped

2 small fresh hot green chillies, sliced

6 cloves garlic, crushed

1 teaspoon finely chopped fresh ginger

1 cinnamon stick

3 green cardamom pods, bruised

5 cloves

1 teaspoon salt

1 tablespoon (20 ml/¾ fl oz) vinegar

2 Indian bay leaves

1 tablespoon (20 ml/¾ fl oz) vegetable oil

10 curry leaves

In a small frying pan, toast the dried chillies, peppercorns, and coriander and cumin seeds for 1 minute. Transfer spices to a grinder, add 2 tablespoons (40 ml/1½ fl oz) water and blend to a paste.

In a large bowl, mix the pork with the spice paste. Add the onions, green chillies, garlic, ginger, cinnamon, cardamom, cloves, salt, vinegar and bay leaves, and mix well. Set aside for 30 minutes. **>**

In a large heavy-based pan heat the vegetable oil and add the pork with its marinade. Stir-fry for a few minutes, add 3 tablespoons (60 ml/2 fl oz) water, bring to the boil, then cover and simmer for 1 hour, stirring occasionally, until meat is cooked. (Add a little more water if necessary.)

Stir in the curry leaves and serve with plain rice.

❧ You can reduce the heat in this curry by using fewer dried chillies and only one fresh chilli.

Pork Vindaloo

Serves 4–6

⅓ cup (80 ml/3 fl oz) vegetable oil

2 onions, chopped

700 g (1 lb/9 oz) pork leg or shoulder, cut into 2-cm (5-in) cubes

6 cloves

8 black peppercorns

6 green cardamom pods, bruised

4 small fresh hot green chillies

1 tablespoon (20 g/¾ oz) soft brown sugar

1 teaspoon salt

1 tablespoon vindaloo curry paste (page 245)

⅓ cup (80 ml/3 fl oz) malt vinegar

Heat the oil in a frying pan over medium heat and fry the onions until soft and golden (about 5 minutes). Add the pork, cloves, peppercorns, cardamom pods and whole chillies, and fry for a few minutes, until the pork is coated with the spices. Then add the sugar and salt, and stir-fry for another 5 minutes. Add the vindaloo paste and cook for 20 minutes, or until the pork is done. Stir in the vinegar and simmer for 5 minutes more.

Remove the whole green chillies and cardamom pods. Serve the curry hot with plain rice.

Goan Pork Curry

Serves 4

4 dried red chillies, crumbled

10 black peppercorns

5 cloves

1 teaspoon cumin seeds

1 cinnamon stick

⅓ cup (80 ml/3 fl oz)
vegetable oil

5-cm (2-in) piece fresh ginger,
grated

6 cloves garlic, crushed

700 g (1 lb 9 oz) lean
pork, cubed

½ teaspoon ground turmeric

1 tablespoon tomato paste

½ teaspoon ground chilli

1 onion, thinly sliced

2 tablespoons (40 ml/1½ fl oz)
white vinegar

1 teaspoon salt

1 teaspoon sugar

2 small fresh hot green
chillies, split open,
for garnish

In a spice grinder or food processor, grind the dried chillies, peppercorns, cloves, cumin seeds and cinnamon stick to a fine powder.

Heat half the oil in a large heavy-based pan and stir-fry the ginger and garlic for 1 minute. Add the prepared spice mix and fry for 30 seconds, being careful not to let the spices burn. Increase the heat, add the pork and turmeric, and stir-fry for 5–6 minutes. Add 1 cup (250 ml/8½ fl oz) warm water, the tomato paste and ground chilli, bring to the boil, cover and then simmer for 30–45 minutes. ❯

Heat the remaining oil in a separate frying pan and fry the onion for about 8 minutes, until well browned. Add onion to the pork mixture and stir, then add the vinegar, salt and sugar, and simmer for another 30 minutes or so, until the pork is tender.

Serve garnished with the green chillies.

Tamarind Spicy Pork

Serves 4

2 small fresh hot green
chillies, deseeded and
chopped

2 onions, chopped

4 cloves garlic, crushed

1 stem lemongrass (bulb end
only), lightly crushed

2 tablespoons tamarind paste

2 tablespoons (40 ml/1½ fl oz)
melted ghee or vegetable oil

1 tablespoon ground coriander

1 teaspoon ground turmeric

1 teaspoon ground cardamom

1 teaspoon ground chilli

1 teaspoon grated fresh ginger

1 cinnamon stick

700 g (1 lb 9 oz) pork fillet, diced

1 cup (250 ml/8½ fl oz)
boiling water

½ cup chopped fresh coriander

sliced fresh red chillies,
for garnish

Place green chillies, onion, garlic, lemongrass and tamarind paste in a food processor and blend until smooth.

Heat the ghee or oil in a heavy-based saucepan. Add the chilli and onion mixture and the ground spices, ginger and cinnamon, and cook for 2 minutes, stirring constantly. Add the pork and cook until lightly browned and well coated with the spice mixture. Pour in hot water, bring to the boil, then reduce heat, cover and simmer for 30 minutes. Uncover and simmer for another 30 minutes, or until pork is tender. Stir in fresh coriander. Garnish with red chillies and serve with plain rice.

Desserts & Drinks

Indian sweet dishes tend to be very sweet. Some of the best-known desserts have their origins in different religions: kheer, a festive pudding-like dish of rice or other grains, was made popular by Hindus; halwa, made with semolina and ghee, is a traditional Muslim dish.

Climate tends to dictate which type of dessert is served at which time of the year. Halwa (halva), being very rich, is traditionally served only in winter. Indian ice-cream (kulfi) is, of course, particularly popular during the long, hot summer months. Kulfi is much easier to make at home than western-style ice-cream.

Lassi (a drink made from yoghurt or buttermilk) is often served with a hot meal. Tea is another favourite beverage and is served in myriad ways. Two drinks available from street vendors all over the country are masala chai (spiced milky tea) and nimbu pani (spicy lemonade).

< Sweet Dumplings (page 204)

Sweet Dumplings

Gulab jamun

Makes 25

vegetable oil for deep-frying

SUGAR SYRUP

5 cups (1.1 kg/2 lb 5 oz) sugar

3 green cardamom pods,
bruised

5 cloves

3 teaspoons rosewater

DUMPLINGS

3 cups milk powder

1 cup (150 g/5 oz) self-raising
flour

⅓ cup (80 ml/3 fl oz) vegetable
oil

200 ml (7 fl oz) full-cream
milk

Make the syrup first. Place the sugar and 5 cups (1.25 L/2 pt 10 fl oz) water in a saucepan with the cardamom and cloves. Bring to the boil over medium heat, then reduce heat and simmer for 10 minutes. Allow to cool, then stir in the rosewater.

Heat the oil over high heat in a wok or other pan suitable for deep-frying, then turn the heat off and let the oil cool down again. (This affects the flavour of the dumplings.)

To prepare the dumplings, sift milk powder and flour into a bowl, add oil and milk, and knead to form a soft dough. Shape the dough into golfball-sized balls and set aside on a greased surface.

Reheat the oil over very low heat, then drop in the balls, a few at a time. Turn them continuously to ensure they cook and colour evenly. Once the dumplings are browned, remove from the oil and drain on paper towels.

Place the dumplings in the cooled syrup, ensuring each is well covered, and set aside for 2–3 hours to allow them to absorb the liquid.

When ready to serve, gently transfer dumplings to a serving dish. They can be served hot or cold (reheat in microwave for 30 seconds if serving hot).

卐 Many traditional Indian desserts involve boiling milk down to its solids. These days, short-cuts to this lengthy process have been introduced, such as using milk powder.

Indian Rice Pudding

Kheer

Serves 4

2 tablespoons basmati rice

1 L (34 fl oz) full-cream milk

pinch of saffron threads

1 green cardamom pod, bruised

¼ cup (55 g/1¾ oz) caster sugar

2 tablespoons sultanas

1 cup ground almonds

½ teaspoon freshly ground nutmeg

3 tablespoons crushed pistachios

4 dried apricots, sliced

Rinse the rice in cold water, then drain.

Heat 2 tablespoons (40 ml/1½ fl oz) of the milk, add saffron threads and set aside to soak for 10 minutes.

Pour remaining milk into a heavy-based saucepan and add the rice, saffron liquid and cardamom pod. Bring to the boil, then reduce heat and simmer for 30–40 minutes, until mixture has thickened slightly. Add the sugar, sultanas and ground almonds and cook for a few minutes.

Remove mixture from the heat and allow to cool, stirring occasionally to incorporate the skin that forms on the surface.

Discard the cardamom pod and divide rice between individual serving dishes. Serve garnished with the nutmeg, pistachios and dried apricots.

Coconut Ice-cream

Nariyal kulfi

Serves 4

1 tablespoon desiccated coconut

½ cup (125 ml/4 fl oz) coconut milk

½ teaspoon ground cardamom

½ cup (125 ml/4 fl oz) condensed milk

1 cup (250 ml/8½ fl oz) cream

Toast the desiccated coconut in a small frying pan for a few minutes and then set aside to cool.

Place all the ingredients, except the cream, in a large bowl and mix thoroughly. Cover with cling wrap and place in fridge to chill for 4–5 hours.

When mixture is very cold, add the cream and whisk until smooth. Spoon into a loaf tin, cover with cling wrap and freeze for at least 3 hours before serving.

☸ Instead of using a loaf tin, you could use traditional metal kulfi moulds, available from Indian grocery stores.

Halwa with Almonds & Pistachios

Serves 6

1 cup (220 g/8 oz) sugar

1 green cardamom pod,
  bruised

70 ml (2½ fl oz) melted ghee

1 cup coarse semolina

1 tablespoon sultanas

½ tablespoon blanched and
  slivered almonds

½ tablespoon pistachios,
  chopped

Place the sugar and 3 cups (750 ml/1½ pt) water in a saucepan with the cardamom and stir over low heat until sugar dissolves. Set aside.

Heat the ghee in a heavy-based saucepan over low heat. Add the semolina and stir constantly until light-brown (about 5 minutes). Remove from heat and set aside to cool.

Add the sultanas and the sugar syrup to the cooled semolina, and stir over a low heat until mixture thickens. Stir in half the almonds and pistachios.

Transfer mixture to a serving dish and garnish with the remaining nuts.

₰ Halwa is probably India's most famous sweet dish. It is made on festive occasions such as birthdays and Diwali, and is taken to Hindu temples as a religious offering.

Carrot Halwa

Serves 8

2 tablespoons (40 ml/1½ fl oz)
  melted ghee

3 kg (6 lb 9 oz) carrots, grated

500 g (1 lb 2 oz) white sugar

4 green cardamom pods,
  bruised

1 L (34 fl oz) full-cream milk

1 tablespoon chopped
  pistachios

Heat the ghee in a large pot, add the grated carrot and cook over low heat
for 10 minutes, stirring often. Add the sugar and the cardamom pods, stir
thoroughly, then pour in the milk and cook for another 5 minutes, with the
lid off, still stirring.

Serve warm, garnished with chopped pistachios.

Vermicelli Milk Pudding

Sevian kheer

Serves 4

2 cups (500 ml/17 fl oz)
full-cream milk

pinch of saffron threads

⅓ cup (80 ml/3 fl oz)
melted ghee

2 teaspoons chopped cashew
nuts, plus extra for garnish

2 teaspoons sultanas

150 g dried vermicelli,
roughly broken

½ cup (90 g/3 oz) lightly
packed soft brown sugar

Heat a tablespoon of the milk, add saffron threads and set aside to soak.

Heat the ghee in a large heavy-based saucepan and fry the cashews and sultanas until golden. Add the vermicelli and fry for a few moments, until lightly coloured but not brown. Add the remaining milk and the sugar, and bring to the boil, stirring continuously. Reduce heat and simmer until the vermicelli is soft and the pudding is fairly thick (around 5 minutes). Add the saffron and its soaking milk and cook for another minute.

Serve hot or cold, garnished with chopped cashews.

❧ This pudding is traditionally eaten by Muslims after the Ramadan fast.

❧ Indian vermicelli is thinner than the Italian version and is available at Indian grocery stores, although Italian vermicelli can be substituted.

Pistachio Ice-Cream

Pista kulfi

Serves 4

½ cup unsalted pistachios,
  plus extra for garnish

1 L (34 fl oz) full-cream milk

1 green cardamom pod,
  bruised

⅓ cup (70 g/2½ oz) caster
  sugar

½ cup (125 ml/4 fl oz) cream

Soak the pistachios in a little of the milk for about 30 minutes.

In a heavy-based saucepan, bring the remaining milk to the boil with the cardamom pod. Reduce heat and simmer until milk is reduced by half (about 20 minutes), stirring constantly.

Drain soaked pistachios, then mash with a fork (or blend briefly in a food processor). Add nuts to the pan along with the sugar. Stir and simmer for 5 minutes, then remove from heat and discard the cardamom pod.

Allow mixture to cool, then place in the refrigerator to chill. After an hour, add the cream and beat mixture with a whisk until it is light. Pour into a loaf tin, cover with cling wrap and freeze until needed.

To serve, remove ice-cream from freezer and allow to defrost slightly, then place in a large bowl and stir well to break up the ice particles. Spoon into individual serving bowls and garnish with chopped pistachios.

Spiced Fruit Salad

Serves 4–6

fresh mint leaves, for garnish

vanilla ice-cream or drained
yoghurt (see page 17),
to serve

SPICED SYRUP

¾ cup (170 g/6 oz) caster
sugar

2 cloves

1 Indian bay leaf

1 cinnamon stick, broken
in half

½ teaspoon fennel seeds

2.5-cm (1-in) piece fresh
ginger, finely chopped

grated zest and juice of
1 orange

grated zest and juice of 1 lime

FRUIT SALAD

1 mango, flesh chopped

1½ cups peeled fresh lychees,
deseeded

1 large pineapple, peeled and
cut into bite-sized chunks

pulp of 4 passionfruits

4 bananas, sliced

To make the syrup, place the sugar, cloves, bay leaf, cinnamon, fennel seeds and ginger in a saucepan along with 2 cups (500 ml/17 fl oz) water. Place over a low heat and stir until the sugar dissolves, then simmer for 10 minutes over medium heat. Remove syrup from the heat and add the orange and lime juices and zest.

Divide the prepared fruit between bowls and drizzle with the syrup. Garnish with mint and serve immediately with ice-cream or yoghurt.

Creamy Yoghurt Dessert

Shrikhand

Serves 4

1 tablespoon (20 ml/¾ fl oz)
full-cream milk

1 teaspoon saffron threads

1 L (34 fl oz) plain yoghurt,
drained (see page 17)

½ cup (110 g/4 oz) caster
sugar

2 tablespoons chopped
pistachios

2 tablespoons chopped
almonds

½ teaspoon freshly grated
nutmeg

½ teaspoon ground cardamom

Heat the milk, add saffron threads and set aside to soak for 20 minutes.

Place the drained yoghurt in a large bowl, add the sugar and beat by hand until well blended. Stir in the saffron milk. Place mixture in a serving bowl and chill for 1 hour.

To serve, sprinkle with the pistachios, almonds, nutmeg and cardamom.

Sago & Coconut Pudding

Sabudana kheer

Serves 4

1 cup sago

2¼ cups (500 ml/17 fl oz)
full-cream milk

½ cup (110 g/4 oz) caster
sugar

½ cup sultanas

pinch of salt

200 ml (7 fl oz) coconut milk

½ teaspoon ground cardamom

2 tablespoons flaked almonds,
for garnish

shredded zest of 1 lime,
for garnish

fresh fruit, to serve

Rinse the sago, drain, then leave to stand for 15 minutes.

Bring the milk to the boil in a large heavy-based saucepan. Reduce the heat, add the sugar and stir over very low heat until dissolved. Stir in the drained sago, the sultanas, salt and coconut milk, and simmer gently for 6–8 minutes until the sago is tender and transparent. Remove from heat and stir in the cardamom.

Pour sago mixture into individual dishes and garnish with the almonds and lime zest. Serve warm or cold, with fresh fruit such as mango.

Besan Burfi

Makes 14

¾ cup (180 ml/6 fl oz) melted
  ghee

1 cup (145 g/5 oz) besan
  (chickpea flour)

1 cup (225 g/8 oz) caster sugar

1 cup chopped unsalted
  almonds or cashews, plus
  extra for garnish

Grease a 20-cm (8-in) square cake tin that has a removable base.

Heat the ghee in a non-stick frying pan and cook besan flour over very low heat, stirring constantly, for 15 minutes. As soon as the flour starts to brown, remove from the heat (be careful it doesn't burn).

Add the sugar and nuts to the flour, and mix well. Return pan to the heat for 1 minute, stirring, then spoon mixture into the prepared tin and press down firmly to smooth the top. Remove the sides of the tin while the mixture is still slightly warm, and sprinkle burfi with extra chopped nuts.

Cut into 2.5-cm (1-in) squares and serve chilled.

Almond Milk Drink

Makes 4 cups

1½ cups almonds

1½ cups unsalted pistachios

1 L (34 fl oz) chilled
   full-cream milk

2 tablespoons (30 g/1 oz)
   caster sugar

½ teaspoon ground cardamom

2 teaspoons rosewater

In a food processor or blender, grind the almonds, pistachios and about 2 teaspoons of the milk to a smooth paste. Add the rest of the milk and the remaining ingredients, and blend well.

Serve chilled, over ice.

Ginger Chai

Serves 2

1½ cups (400 ml/13½ fl oz)
  milk

2 teaspoons black tea leaves

2 teaspoons caster sugar

2.5-cm (1-in) piece fresh
  ginger, peeled

Bring the milk and ½ cup (125 ml/4 fl oz) water to the boil in a saucepan.
Lower heat and add the tea leaves, sugar and ginger. Simmer, stirring, for
2 minutes or until the tea is desired colour. Strain, and serve immediately.

❧ For a more intense ginger flavour, grate the ginger before adding.

Spicy Lemonade

Nimbu pani

Serves 4

**1 tablespoon (15 g/½ oz)
caster sugar**

**½ cup (125 ml/4 fl oz) freshly
squeezed lemon juice**

2 teaspoons black salt

handful of fresh mint leaves

handful of ice cubes

lemon wedges, for garnish

Mix 4 cups (1 L/34 fl oz) cold water with the sugar in a large saucepan and stir over high heat until sugar dissolves. Add the lemon juice, black salt, mint leaves and ice cubes, and allow to cool. Chill. Serve with a lemon wedge.

Black salt is a pinkish-grey rock salt with a distinctive mineral taste, much used as a flavouring and condiment in Indian cookery. It is available in powdered or crystal form, from Indian food stores.

Pistachio Lassi

Serves 6–8

¾ cup pistachios, plus extra
for garnish

1 teaspoon pista essence
(optional)

3 cups (750 ml/1½ pt)
plain yoghurt

½ cup (110 g/4 oz) caster
sugar

handful of ice cubes

Place pistachios in a food processor and grind to a fine powder. Combine
with the other ingredients and blend until frothy.

Serve immediately, garnished with chopped pistachios.

- Pista essence is a green food colouring sometimes flavoured with
  pistachio. It is available at Indian food stores.
- To make a mango lassi, blend the flesh of 2 mangoes with 1 cup (250 ml/
  8½ fl oz) milk, 1 cup yoghurt, a handful of ice cubes, a tablespoon of
  sugar and ½ teaspoon ground cardamom.

Extras

Every Indian meal includes at least one chutney or pickle. Designed to complement and add interest to a dish, these accompaniments may be sweet or sour, fruity and mild, or very hot or tangy – most are pungent and a little can go a long, long way. Like much Indian food, chutneys and pickles reflect regional influences in the choice of spices and other flavourings. In South India, for example, they are likely to include mustard seeds and tamarind.

Fresh chutneys and relishes are quick and easy to make at home, although they must be used within 2–3 days. As well as vinegar-based chutneys for keeping, Indian cooks also make a range of pickles, which often include oil (typically mustard oil) as well as spices and other flavourings. A raita, made of chopped or grated vegetables mixed with yoghurt and mild spices, makes a cooling sauce, side-dish or dip to accompany hot foods.

< Fresh Coriander Relish (page 226)

Fresh Coriander Relish

Serves 4–6

3 cups fresh coriander leaves

1 onion, chopped

1 clove garlic, chopped

1 fresh hot green chilli,
chopped

1 teaspoon salt

2 teaspoons sugar

2 teaspoons freshly squeezed
lemon juice

In a food processor, blend all the ingredients with ½ cup (125 ml/4 fl oz) water to form a paste. Adjust seasoning to taste.

Serve chilled, with meat dishes.

This chutney will keep for 2–3 days in the fridge.

Cucumber Raita

Serves 4–6

1 teaspoon cumin seeds

1 cup (250 ml/8½ fl oz) plain
  yoghurt, lightly whisked

1 Continental cucumber,
  deseeded and finely chopped

2 tablespoons chopped
  fresh mint

salt and freshly ground
  black pepper

Toast the cumin seeds in a small frying pan until they start to crackle. Remove from heat and grind to a fine powder.

Place yoghurt in a bowl with all the other ingredients (reserve a little of the cucumber and mint for garnish). Mix well and season to taste with salt and pepper.

Serve chilled, garnished with the reserved cucumber and mint.

Use within 1–2 days.

    The cucumber for a raita is commonly peeled before adding, but this is not strictly necessary.

Fresh Coconut Chutney

Makes 2 cups

1 tablespoon yellow lentils (toor dal)

flesh from ½ fresh coconut

3 cloves garlic, chopped

5-cm (2-in) piece fresh ginger, sliced

2 small fresh hot green chillies, chopped

½ cup fresh coriander

2 tablespoons (40 ml/1½ fl oz) freshly squeezed lemon juice

2 cups (500 ml/17 fl oz) plain yoghurt

1 teaspoon salt

½ teaspoon garam masala

2 tablespoons (40 ml/1½ fl oz) vegetable oil

2 small fresh hot red chillies

6 curry leaves

2 teaspoons black mustard seeds

2 teaspoons ground fenugreek

½ teaspoon ground paprika

Rinse the lentils and soak for 10 minutes in enough cold water to cover. Drain and set aside.

Cut the coconut flesh into small pieces and place in food processor with the garlic, ginger, green chillies, coriander, lemon juice and 2 tablespoons (40 ml/1½ fl oz) water. Process to a coarse paste, then place in a large bowl and stir in the yoghurt, salt and garam masala. Mix well and set aside.

Heat the oil in a heavy-based pan, add the whole red chillies and curry leaves, and stir-fry for 20 seconds. Add the drained lentils and fry over low heat for 3–4 minutes, until browned. Remove from heat, place in a dish and leave to cool.

In the same frying pan, fry the mustard seeds for 30 seconds, then add the lentil mixture, fenugreek and paprika. Cook for another 30 seconds, add the coconut–yoghurt mixture and stir well to combine.

Serve cold with any South Indian dishes, such as stuffed pancakes (page 56) or fish molee (page 125).

This chutney will keep for 2–3 days in the fridge.

Onion & Mint Chutney

Serves 4

4 onions, chopped

1 cup chopped fresh mint

1 cup chopped fresh coriander

**2 teaspoons chopped fresh
ginger**

2 teaspoons chopped garlic

1 teaspoon sugar

**1 teaspoon freshly squeezed
lemon juice**

1 teaspoon salt

Place all the ingredients in a food processor with 1 tablespoon (20 ml/
¾ fl oz) water and grind to a thick paste. Adjust seasonings to taste.

Serve cold with fried foods such as onion bhajis (page 32).

This chutney will keep for 2–3 days in the fridge.

Mango Chutney

Makes about 1 cup

1 large mango, flesh cubed

juice of 1 lemon

2 tablespoons (40 ml/1½ fl oz)
white-wine vinegar

½ teaspoon crushed dried
red chillies

1 teaspoon cumin seeds,
toasted

¼ teaspoon nigella seeds

3 cloves

4 black peppercorns

1 teaspoon salt

½ cup (90 g/3 oz) lightly
packed soft brown sugar

2.5-cm (1-in) piece fresh
ginger, thinly sliced

1 clove garlic, crushed

1 teaspoon shredded lemon
or orange zest

Place the mango in a ceramic bowl with the lemon juice and set aside.

Pour vinegar into a saucepan and add the chillies, cumin and nigella seeds,
cloves, peppercorns, salt and sugar. Simmer for 15 minutes. Add mango,
ginger, garlic and zest, and simmer until mango is mushy (about 10 minutes). Remove from heat and cool completely. Transfer to a sterilised jar and
chill for 3 days before serving.

The chutney will keep for 1–2 months in the refrigerator or a cool place.

Nigella seeds (onion seeds, wild onion seeds, kalonji) – the dried fruit of
a small annual herb – are used in fish dishes, pickles and spice mixes.

Tomato Chutney

Makes 2–4 cups

1 kg (2 lb 3 oz) tomatoes, peeled and chopped

1 cup (220 g/8 oz) caster sugar

¾ cup (180 ml/6 fl oz) malt vinegar

3 tablespoons (60 ml/2 fl oz) freshly squeezed lemon juice

4 cloves garlic, finely chopped

2.5-cm (1-in) piece fresh ginger

2 red chillies, quartered and deseeded

1 teaspoon salt

1 teaspoon garam masala

2 tablespoons (40 ml/1½ fl oz) mustard oil

2 small fresh hot green chillies

1 teaspoon fenugreek seeds

1 teaspoon cumin seeds

1 teaspoon yellow mustard seeds

Place the tomatoes in a large heavy-based saucepan, add the sugar, vinegar and lemon juice, and bring to the boil. Add the garlic, ginger, red chillies and salt, lower the heat and simmer for 45 minutes, or until the mixture has the consistency of a thin jam. Add the garam masala, stir well, then remove pan from heat and allow to cool.

Heat the mustard oil in a heavy-based frying pan over high heat until it starts to smoke. Remove from the heat, add the whole green chillies and remaining spices, and stir-fry for 10 seconds. Pour the spiced oil over the chutney mixture and mix well.

Cool chutney completely before pouring into sterilised jars.

Keep in the fridge for up to 1 month.

- It is important to smoke the mustard oil before adding the spices, or it will have a bitter taste.
- To make a garlic chutney, crumble 2 dried red chillies and soak in 2 tablespoons (40 ml/1½ fl oz) warm water for 2 minutes. Blend the chillies and soaking water with 5 cloves garlic, 150 g (5 oz) desiccated coconut, 1 teaspoon salt and 2 teaspoons tamarind paste. Serve chilled, with vegetable curries. (Will keep for 2–3 days in the fridge.)

Hot Lime Pickle

Makes 1½ cups

15 limes

1 cup salt

2 tablespoons ground
fenugreek

2 tablespoons mustard powder

¾ cup ground chilli

1 tablespoon ground turmeric

1 cup (250 ml/8½ fl oz)
mustard oil

½ teaspoon asafoetida

1 tablespoon crushed yellow
mustard seeds

Wash the limes thoroughly and then cut each into 8 wedges. Place in a large sterilised jar, add the salt, seal the jar and leave in a warm place for 10 days, until the limes are soft and brown.

Mix together the fenugreek, mustard powder, ground chilli and turmeric, and add to the limes. Stir well, then seal jar again and leave for another 2 days.

Heat the mustard oil in a frying pan over high heat until the oil starts to smoke. Remove from the heat and quickly fry the asafoetida and mustard seeds. Pour this spicy oil over the limes and mix well. Seal jar and leave in a warm place for 1 week before using.

This pickle will keep for 2–3 weeks in the fridge.

Green Chilli & Garlic Pickle

Makes about 2 cups

⅓ cup crushed yellow
mustard seeds

⅓ cup cumin seeds, toasted
and crushed

¼ cup ground turmeric

⅓ cup crushed garlic

180 ml (6 fl oz) white vinegar

⅓ cup (75 g/2½ oz) white sugar

2 teaspoons salt

⅔ cup (5½ fl oz) mustard oil

20 cloves garlic, peeled

500 g (1 lb 2 oz) small fresh
hot green chillies, halved
and stems removed

In a glass bowl, mix together the mustard and cumin seeds, turmeric, crushed garlic, vinegar, sugar and salt. Cover, and set aside for 30 minutes.

Heat the mustard oil in a frying pan over high heat until it smokes, then remove from heat, add the spice mixture and fry over low heat for about 5 minutes. Stir in the garlic cloves, increase the heat and cook for a further 5 minutes. Add the green chillies, lower the heat and cook gently for 30 minutes, until the chillies are soft.

Cool completely before transferring to sterilised jars. Leave for a week before using.

This pickle is very good with vegetable curries. It will last for 2–3 weeks in the fridge.

Tandoori Masala

Makes about ¼ cup

2 teaspoons cumin seeds

2 teaspoons coriander seeds

1 cinnamon stick

1 teaspoon cloves

1 teaspoon ground chilli

1 teaspoon ground ginger

1 teaspoon ground turmeric

1 teaspoon garlic powder

1 teaspoon salt

½ teaspoon red food colouring powder

Toast the whole spices in a wok or saucepan over medium heat until they start to smoke. Allow to cool, then combine with the ground chilli, ginger, turmeric, garlic, salt and food colouring, and blend in an electric grinder.

Store the spice mix for up to 6 months in an airtight jar.

ॐ Red food colouring in powdered form is available from Indian grocery stores.

Chana Masala

Makes about 1½ tablespoons

2 teaspoons cumin seeds

1 teaspoon coriander seeds

2 cloves

2 dried red chillies, crumbled

4 black peppercorns

2 green cardamom pods

½ teaspoon ground ginger

½ teaspoon mango powder (amchoor)

In a frying pan over low heat, toast the cumin, coriander, cloves, red chillies, peppercorns and cardamom pods for a few minutes, stirring continuously. Transfer to a spice grinder and add the ginger and mango powder. Grind together to form a powder.

This mix can be stored in an airtight container in the fridge for 2–3 weeks.

❧ Chana masala is a special blend of spices designed for use in chickpea dishes; it may include more than a dozen spices. It can be bought from Indian food stores.

Mild Curry Powder

Makes about 1 cup

½ cup coriander seeds

4 tablespoons cumin seeds

2 tablespoons fennel seeds

1 tablespoon fenugreek seeds

3 small dried red chillies

5 dried curry leaves

1 tablespoon ground chilli

½ tablespoon ground turmeric

½ teaspoon salt

In a wok or large pan over low heat, toast the coriander, cumin, fennel and fenugreek seeds with the red chillies and curry leaves for 8–10 minutes, stirring continuously until the spices darken. Allow to cool.

Place the toasted whole spices in a spice or coffee grinder and grind to a fine powder. Add the ground chilli, turmeric and salt, and mix well.

Store in an airtight container in a cool dark place for 2–4 months.

This is a mild curry powder but you could boost the heat by increasing the quantity of dried chillies.

Mild Curry Paste

Makes about 2½ cups

½ cup coriander seeds

4 tablespoons cumin seeds

2 tablespoons fennel seeds

1 tablespoon fenugreek seeds

3 small dried red chillies

5 dried curry leaves

1 tablespoon ground chilli

½ tablespoon ground turmeric

⅔ cup (150 ml/5 fl oz) white-wine vinegar

1 cup (250 ml/8 fl oz) vegetable oil

In a spice or coffee grinder, grind the coriander, cumin, fennel and fenugreek seeds with the red chillies and curry leaves. Transfer to a bowl and add the ground chilli and turmeric. Mix well. Add the vinegar and ⅓ cup (80 ml/3 fl oz) water and stir to form a thin paste.

Heat the vegetable oil in a wok or large frying pan and stir-fry the spice paste until all water has evaporated (about 10 minutes). Allow to cool slightly, then transfer to an airtight jar.

This curry paste will keep for 3–4 weeks in the refrigerator.

This is a mild curry paste but you can increase the heat by adding more dried red chillies.

Vindaloo Curry Paste

Makes 1 cup

1 tablespoon cumin seeds

4 dried red chillies, crumbled

4 cloves

1 teaspoon black peppercorns

3 cardamom pods, bruised

1 teaspoon black
mustard seeds

1 teaspoon garlic powder

1 teaspoon ground fenugreek

1 teaspoon sugar

⅓ cup (80 ml/3 fl oz)
white-wine vinegar

2 tablespoons (40 ml/1½ fl oz)
vegetable oil

In a mortar or spice grinder, grind the cumin, chillies, cloves, peppercorns, cardamom pods and black mustard seeds to a powder. Transfer to a bowl and stir in the garlic powder, fenugreek and sugar. Add the white-wine vinegar and 1 tablespoon (20 ml/¾ fl oz) water and stir to form a thin paste.

Heat the oil in a large frying pan or wok and stir-fry the spice mixture over low heat until all the water has evaporated (about 10 minutes). Leave to cool before transferring to an airtight glass jar.

This curry paste will keep for 3–4 weeks in the refrigerator.

Special Ingredients

AJWAIN Sometimes called carom, this seed looks like a miniature cumin seed and has a fragrance similar to thyme. It is used in tandoori spice mixes, some rice dishes, and pickles and chutneys. Caraway or celery seeds can be substituted.

AMCHUR A sour-tasting powder made from ground unripe mangoes. It is used in some vegetables dishes, in pickles and chutneys, and sometimes as a garnish.

ANISEED An aromatic seed with a fresh, bitter-sweet, liquorice-like taste. It may be used to flavour rich meat curries or heated in oil then drizzled over lentil dishes. Powdered aniseed is sometimes used in Indian sweets.

ASAFOETIDA A gum that comes from dried sap, it is often added to vegetable and lentil dishes as a seasoning and anti-flatulent. It is available as lumps or in ground form, and should be used sparingly.

BESAN (chickpea flour, gram flour) This flour, made from dried chickpeas, is used in many Indian breads and other dishes. It is available at supermarkets and Indian food stores.

CARDAMOM Both green and black cardamom pods are used in Indian cooking. **Green cardamom** is a spice that is native to India. It has a sweet flavour with a mild, pleasant aroma and is used in both savoury and sweet dishes. The pods should be lightly bruised (hit once or twice with a pestle) to release the flavour of the seeds, before being toasted or added to dishes. **Black cardamom** is larger and has a more intense flavour than green cardamom. It is often added to meat dishes, and is usually toasted first. Always remove from a dish before serving, as it can form a choking hazard. Both green and black cardamom are best stored in pod form to preserve the flavour of the seeds inside.

CHILLIES Chillies come in all shapes and sizes, with varying degrees of heat. Indian recipes call for chillies belonging to the *Capsicum frutescens* species. These are sometimes called finger chillies or bird's eye chillies. Mexican varieties such as jalapeno are not suited to Indian cooking.

Fresh, unripe chillies come in various shades of green, while the ripe fruits are red. The flavour and aroma of red and green chillies varies slightly, so it is best not to interchange the two. Indian green chillies can be just as hot, if not hotter than red ones.

The level of heat in a chilli depends on the amount of capsaicin present in the seeds, and small chillies are often hotter than large ones. Contrary to popular belief, heat from chillies is not diminished by cooking. **Ground chilli** (red chilli powder or *lal mirch*) is very hot and should be handled carefully. **Dried chillies** are often crumbled, then fried with other spices, or ground and added to spice mixes. For tips on handling and using chillies, see page 11.

COCONUT MILK Coconut products bring a smooth creaminess to curry sauces. The white flesh of ripe coconuts is grated and squeezed to extract coconut cream, which in turn is infused with water to produce coconut milk. Canned coconut cream and milk is ready to use; creamed coconut, a concentrated form sold in blocks, is grated or chopped and mixed with water before use; coconut milk powder is mixed into warm water. See page 12 for how to make coconut milk or cream from desiccated coconut or fresh coconut.

CURRY LEAVES These leaves, from a South-East Asian tree, are similar in appearance to bay leaves but impart a different, particularly aromatic, flavour to dishes. They are widely used in southern and western Indian cooking. It's worth looking for the fresh leaves, which are often found in the refrigerated sections of Asian and Indian food stores, although dried ones can be substituted.

FENUGREEK The yellowish-brown seeds of this annual herb are one of the most distinctively flavoured Indian spices and are used sparingly. The leaves (fresh and dried) are also included in a number of Indian dishes. The seeds are widely available, while the leaves can often be found in produce markets and Indian and Middle Eastern food stores.

GARLIC POWDER Dried garlic powder (not to be confused with garlic salt) is dried garlic that has been ground to a fine powder. It is available in the spice section of supermarkets.

GARAM MASALA This aromatic blend of ground spices is used as a seasoning or spicy garnish. Recipes are often handed down from generation to generation, but most varieties contain coriander, cumin, peppercorns, cloves, cardamom, cinnamon and nutmeg. It is available in supermarkets and Indian food stores.

GHEE A golden, nutty-flavoured form of clarified butter, which keeps well and won't burn at high temperatures. It's widely available in supermarkets, and Asian and Indian food stores, but you can easily make it yourself (see page 13). Oil or butter can be used instead of ghee in some recipes, but many Indian breads, desserts and other dishes rely on the rich taste of ghee.

GRAM FLOUR *see* besan

INDIAN BAY LEAVES These leaves come from the Indian cassia tree and have an aroma like cinnamon. They are used to add aroma to a dish, not to flavour it. They are similar to western bay leaves and these can be substituted in recipes. You can buy Indian bay leaves in Indian grocery stores.

KOKUM This purplish-black sticky dried fruit is used in South Indian dishes as a souring agent. It is usually available (in Asian and Indian food stores) in the form of dried rind, which is soaked in water before use. Lemon juice or tamarind can be substituted.

LENTILS These legumes are available in numerous varieties. Whole **black lentils** (urad dal, black gram) are black with flecks of grey and have a rich taste. Split black lentils (white lentils) are white and have a more subtle taste. Whole **red lentils** (masoor dal) are dark-brown to greenish-black, while split red lentils are orangey-red. The whole lentils are chewy and coarse, have a stronger taste and take longer to cook than the split version. **Yellow lentils** (toor dal, yellow split peas) are yellow in colour and are sold split into round halves. They are easy to digest and have a subtle nutty flavour. You can substitute **gram lentils** (chana dal), which are slightly bigger and coarser.

Gram lentils are split black chickpeas, and are the most widely grown dal in India. They have a stronger flavour than most other varieties. **Mung beans** (moong dal, green gram) are oval-shaped and green when whole. When split they are flattened and yellow. Whole mung beans have a stronger flavour than the split ones and are rather chewy.

MANGO POWDER *see* amchur

MUSTARD SEEDS There are three main varieties of mustard seed: yellow, brown and black. **Yellow** (raw) mustard seeds have almost no smell but once cooked have a distinctive flavour and contain a lot of heat; use sparingly. Yellow mustard seeds are sometimes used in pickles and chutneys. **Black** and **brown** mustard seeds are more pungent than the yellow ones and are often used in curries.

PANEER A simple, unripened Indian cheese with the consistency of cottage cheese or tofu. It is available at supermarkets and Indian food stores. To make your own paneer, see recipe page 15.

RICE FLOUR Rice flour is made from very finely ground rice grains. It is most often used to make doughs and batters, particularly in South India.

TAMARIND This sticky brown fruit pulp is used as a souring agent in many Indian dishes (though it is fruity rather than bitter). You can buy it as a ready-made paste, which just needs to be diluted with water. (It is also available in compressed slabs, but this form is more fiddly to prepare, requiring soaking, mashing and straining.) The paste is available in supermarkets, and Asian and Indian food stores.

Conversions

Important note: All cup and spoon measures given in this book are based on Australian standards. The most important thing to remember is that an Australian cup = 250 ml, while an American cup = 237 ml and a British cup = 284 ml. Also, an Australian tablespoon is equivalent to 4 teaspoons, not 3 teaspoons as in the United States and Britain. US equivalents have been provided throughout for all liquid cup/spoon measures. Equivalents for dry ingredients measured in cups/spoons have been included for flour, sugar and rising agents such as baking powder. For other dry ingredients (chopped vegetables, nuts, etc.), American cooks should be generous with their cup measures – slight variations in quantities of such ingredients are unlikely to affect results.

VOLUME

Australian cups/spoons	Millilitres	US fluid ounces
*1 teaspoon	5 ml	
1 tablespoon (4 teaspoons)	20 ml	¾ fl oz
1½ tablespoons	30 ml	1 fl oz
2 tablespoons	40 ml	1½ fl oz
¼ cup	60 ml	2 fl oz
⅓ cup	80 ml	3 fl oz
½ cup	125 ml	4 fl oz
¾ cup	180 ml	6 fl oz
1 cup	250 ml	8½ fl oz
4 cups	1 L	34 fl oz

*the volume of a teaspoon is the same around the world

>

SIZE

Centimetres	Inches
1 cm	⅜ in
2 cm	¾ in
2.5 cm	1 in
5 cm	2 in
10 cm	4 in
15 cm	6 in
20 cm	8 in
30 cm	12 in

TEMPERATURE

Celsius	Fahrenheit
150°C	300°F
160°C	320°F
170°C	340°F
180°C	360°F
190°C	375°F
200°C	390°F
210°C	410°F
220°C	420°F

WEIGHT

Grams	Ounces
15 g	½ oz
30 g	1 oz
60 g	2 oz
85 g	3 oz
110 g	4 oz
140 g	5 oz
170 g	6 oz
200 g	7 oz
225 g	8 oz (½ lb)
450 g	16 oz (1 lb)
500 g	1 lb 2 oz
900 g	2 lb
1 kg	2 lb 3 oz

Index

LONDON, NEW YORK, MUNICH,
MELBOURNE and DELHI

First published in Great Britain in 2011 by
Dorling Kindersley, 80 Strand, London, WC2R 0RL

A Penguin Company

Published by Penguin Group (Australia), 2010
250 Camberwell Road, Camberwell, Victoria 3124, Australia
(a division of Pearson Australia Group Pty Ltd)

10 9 8 7 6 5 4 3 2 1

Design by Claire Tice and Marley Flory © Penguin Group (Australia)
Photography by Julie Renouf
Food styling by Lee Blaylock
Typeset in Nimbus Sans Novus by Post Pre-press Group, Brisbane, Queensland
Scanning and separations by Splitting Image P/L, Clayton, Victoria
Printed and bound in China by Everbest Printing Co. Ltd

A CIP catalogue record for this book is available from the British Library.

ISBN: 978-1-4053-6325-9

Discover more at www.dk.com